Delicious
Places

New Food Culture,
Restaurants, and Interiors

gestalten

TABLE OF CONTENTS

04–07   *INTRODUCTION:*
Doubling Down on Deliciousness

08–15 BRIDGING CULTURES BUILDING COMMUNITIES

16–19   Sala Equis
20–21   Spiritland
22–27   The Blind Donkey
28–31   La Recyclerie
32–33   Benedict

EATRIP:
34–41   Dishes Filled with Love

42–43   Vollpension
44–47   Piada
48–53   Ryù
54–57   Legacy Records

DEUS CAFÉ:
58–65   More Than Just Machines

66–73 WHAT WILL BE ON OUR PLATES TOMORROW?

74–77   Casaplata
78–79   Naim
80–85   Persijn Restaurant and Juniper & Kin
86–89   Tacofino Oasis

KITCHENTOWN:
90–95   Bringing Innovation to the World of Food

96–97   Prossima Fermata
98–101   Poke Poke
102–105   Egg Kneipe
106–111   Pink Zebra
112–113   Atoboy
114–117   Doot Doot Doot & Flaggerdoot

BIG MAMMA:
118–125   Big, Bigger, Biggest

126–133 CELEBRATING CULINARY TRADITIONS

134–137	Astair
138–139	Duddell's
140–145	Prado Restaurante
146–149	La Colmada

LINA STORES:
150–157   Soho's Little Italy

158–161	Aimo e Nadia Bistro
162–163	Crème de la Crème
164–167	21 Gramm

DRAGSHOLM SLOT:
168–175   Raw, Pure, Local

176–179	Mosquito Supper Club
180–181	China Chilcano
182–185	Patent Pending

RYUICHI SAKAMOTO:
186–195   Annoyed by Restaurant Playlists,
a Master Musician Made His Own

196–203 GO GREEN IN THE KITCHEN

204–207	Väkst
208–209	Salad Jungle
210–215	Babel
216–217	Kiin Kiin Bao Bao

MIL:
218–225   High-Altitude Dining

226–229	Graanmarkt 13
230–231	Bazaar Mar
232–235	Farmacy

STEDSANS IN THE WOODS:
236–243   Into the Woods

244–249	Noma
250–253	La Ménagère
254–255	Index
256	Imprint

DOUBLING DOWN ON DELICIOUSNESS

5

From extraordinary locations
to hyper-local cuisine,
a new wave of bars and
restaurants are taking global
gastronomy to increasingly
exciting heights.

"Where should we eat tonight?" It's an age-old question, and one that seems to be getting harder to answer—in a good way. Thankfully, contemporary cuisine is much more than avocado toast, as restaurants around the world continue to push the boundaries of flavor. As a consequence, global gastronomy has never felt more exciting, nor have dining options been more interesting.

The reasons are abundantly clear: they include a burgeoning interest in food cultures and cuisines; the rise of "destination dining," as restaurants seek to stand out from the crowd through dazzling design and architecture; and the explosion of the sustainable food movement, with more and more chefs choosing to use local and seasonal ingredients, serving food that's good for both people and the planet. *Delicious Places* celebrates numerous bars, cafés, and restaurants around the world that typify this exciting new trend in food culture. As the title suggests, they are all places that double down on deliciousness. This means going beyond what's on the plate and showing respect not just for one's ingredients, but also for one's local community

and heritage. In other words, they are places that are exploring the past in order to shape the future.

Consider Mil restaurant, the latest venture from Peruvian star chef Virgilio Martínez Véliz: it takes destination dining to a new level— quite literally. Located in the Andes Mountains, some 11,500 feet (3,500 meters) above sea level, Mil sources all of its ingredients locally, importing nothing. Working with native crops and grains, Martínez makes everything from scratch—even his own chocolate and distilled spirits.

I live in Copenhagen, which often feels like the wellspring of today's food culture. Mil's hyper-localism certainly has echoes of New Nordic cuisine, the culinary movement pioneered by the Copenhagen restaurant Noma more than a decade ago. The movement emerged after years of dominance by molecular gastronomy, which seemed to want to manipulate ingredients and dishes beyond the point of recognition. If molecular gastronomy took a tomato and made it resemble meat, New Nordic takes the opposite approach: the tomato stands on its own and is the tastiest tomato the diner will have ever eaten. In fact, I once ate the most "carroty" carrot I've ever tasted at Amass, the Copenhagen restaurant founded by Matt Orlando, a former head chef at Noma. He once told me that the New Nordic movement was about having an "intense respect for ingredients" and wanting to "pay homage" to them. And while New Nordic cuisine changed Copenhagen's culinary scene beyond recognition— and helped spread the Scandinavian design aesthetic that typifies many of its restaurants (think: natural fibers and neutral accents)—its legacy is bigger still. If your local bistro serves heirloom tomatoes alongside anything foraged or fermented, chances are the kitchen was influenced by Noma. Its ideas have gone global.

Just look at the philosophy at Lisbon's farm-to-table restaurant Prado: "If it's not in season, it's not on the table." While the decor is elegant yet minimalist—pale wooden tables, forest-green accents, sleek pendant light fixtures—the kitchen pays tribute to the Portuguese larder: mouth-watering menu highlights have included hispi cabbage with goat-cheese whey and walnuts; Iberian pork tenderloin with quince and chocolate peppers; and acorn ice cream with pearl barley and dulse.

Prado's owners were inspired by the restaurant's location: a former factory that was derelict and overrun with vegetation when they found it. Cleverly, they preserved some of the original elements, including abandoned machinery that was restored and reassembled—lending Prado an unpretentious vibe and creating a memorable sense of place that's important to any eatery. It is also one of many extraordinary places in *Delicious Places*, which includes a Cantonese restaurant located in a seventeenth-century London church, and a fine-dining spot in an old Manhattan recording studio.

New Nordic lives on in the DNA of restaurants such as Prado and in the ambition of many of today's movers and shakers—like the Copenhagen chef Christian Puglisi, whose 74-acre Farm of Ideas outside the Danish capital provides his four restaurants with meat, dairy, and vegetables. He modeled Farm of Ideas on Dan Barber's Stone Barns Center for Food and Agriculture in New York, which is now in its 15th year of trying to change the way America eats by promoting farm-driven cuisine. In a similar vein, Puglisi hopes to make Farm of Ideas a hub for education about sustainable food systems and a gathering point for producers, farmers, and chefs. It also makes a scrumptious mozzarella, which is best enjoyed on a pizza at Puglisi's Copenhagen pizzeria, Bæst.

In this way, Farm of Ideas represents not only the future of food but also what we might call the holistic restaurant movement—one that cares about its impact on the planet, about the value of community, heritage, and tradition, about respecting ingredients, and about making that tricky question, "Where should we eat tonight?" a little easier for us all.

James Clasper is a journalist based in Copenhagen. He writes about food, design, sustainability, and Scandinavian culture. His work has appeared in the New York Times, the Guardian, and the Financial Times, among other publications.

BRIDGING CULTURES

BUILDING COMMUNITIES

9 From exotic meals prepared for hungry travelers to cooking classes offered by refugees, whether in Berlin or Brooklyn, the culinary world abounds with people driven by the same desire: to build stronger communities and span cultures and generations through the time-honored tradition of getting strangers to break bread together.

Every evening at six o'clock, about two hundred people flow through the large double doors at the entrance of Absalon, a converted church in Copenhagen's Vesterbro neighborhood, find a seat at one of its 27 long tables, and sit down for dinner with strangers. The food is homey, comforting—chili con carne, say, or mushroom risotto—and served "family style" to encourage conversation around the table. Indeed, at Absalon's nightly *fællesspisning*—or communal meal—where people from all walks of life are welcome, strangers fast become friends.

What attracts many people to Absalon every evening—besides the tasty and affordable food—is the opportunity to meet other people and forge new friendships. And no wonder: sharing food is one of the simplest pleasures in life. And while social media might provide a sense of community and a connection to others, when it comes to bridging cultures and building communities, is there really any substitute for sitting down and breaking bread with people?

Perhaps the desire for company and companionship explains the rise of pop-up dinners and supper clubs, too. In our highly atomized, deeply divided world, few things open doors or bring people together quite like food. And where better to share stories about culture, society, and tradition than around the dinner table?

After all, food is a language that everybody understands.

The desire to gather for food may also explain the growing number of street-food markets around the world, from Brooklyn's Smorgasburg to London's Street Feast to Copenhagen's Reffen. These down-to-earth gastronomic hubs are flourishing for many reasons, from the extraordinary range of cuisines they offer to the way they've helped democratize the industry by giving budding chefs a way to prove their concept and test their mettle without the risk of opening a brick-and-mortar café or restaurant. More than that, though, street food markets are all about community—the one forged between stall holders and the one generated with customers. Indeed, the opportunity to speak directly to chefs and exchange stories about dishes and recipes surely contributes to the immense charm of street-food markets.

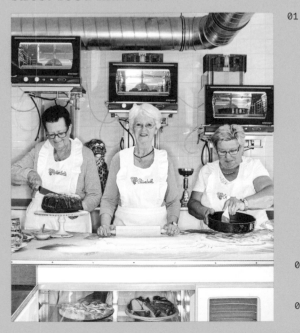

01

The Connecting Link

Pam Warhurst has described her idea for the food-growing initiative Incredible Edible as coming to her "like a bolt from the blue." She was sitting on a train from London to Manchester when she decided to put local food at the heart of her community in Todmorden, a leafy village in northern England. Now more than a decade old, Incredible Edible is dedicated to growing food locally by planting food on unused land. In Todmorden today, orchards grow alongside playing fields, and herb gardens sprout beside bus shelters. As well as encouraging residents of the village to grow food in public spaces, Incredible Edible encourages them to share any relevant skills and support local businesses. Thus, it is not only an example of building communities through the power of food but also of supporting local initiatives.

02

The idea behind Vollpension, a café in the Austrian capital of Vienna, is equally simple: "Who makes the best cake or the tastiest soup? Grandma, of course." Founded in 2012 by social entrepreneur Hannah Lux, Vollpension employs senior

01 The grandmotherly approach taken at Vollpension guarantees the best family recipes while also reinforcing connections across the generations.

02 Since its inception in 2008, Incredible Edible has influenced the establishment of 100 groups in the U.K. and 600 worldwide.

citizens in the kitchen. One purpose is to help combat loneliness and poverty in old age. Inevitably, too, the food served at Vollpension is pretty good. After all, with a lifetime of cooking under their belts, most grandmothers know how to make dishes full of love. But Vollpension is also about community, about bringing many different people together. In this respect, it's a social project that bridges cultures and generations while providing a gateway to other people's lives through food.

"A warm, seasonal, and delicious meal shared at a table with others is much more than the sum of its ingredients," says Lara Gilmore, the wife of Italian star chef Massimo Bottura. "It is a gesture of love." The couple founded Food For Soul, a not-for-profit initiative that sets up community kitchens around the world to help combat food waste while promoting social inclusion. To date, Food for Soul has launched four such kitchens, including Refettorio Felix at St. Cuthbert's, a community kitchen in west London that offers lunch to homeless people and other socially isolated individuals. In fact, each month Refettorio transforms more than 2,000 lb. (1,200 kg) of so-called food waste into 1,100 nourishing meals. Bottura, whose Modena restaurant Osteria Francescana boasts three Michelin stars, says: "The gesture of sitting down to a meal and breaking bread together is the first step toward rebuilding dignity and creating community."

03

Über den Tellerrand takes its name from a German expression for open-mindedness. In particular, the initiative aims to help refugees integrate into society, create a sense of belonging, inclusivity and compassion, and reduce prejudice.

03 Following its success in Berlin, Über den Tellerrand established a mobile unit to spread its culinary ethos across the country.

Food as a Universal Language

"When several refugees set up camp at Oranienplatz in Berlin in 2013, four students thought about how best to get in touch with the local people," says Katja Elsner about the origins of Über den Tellerrand, an initiative that uses food as a portal to different cultures. "So they took a gas stove and food with them to Oranienplatz and simply started cooking with the people."

Literally meaning "beyond your plate," Über den Tellerrand takes its name from a German expression for open-mindedness. In particular, the initiative aims to help refugees and other newcomers integrate into society and develop a sense of belonging. The initiative also tries to encourage inclusivity

05

and compassion in the surrounding community in hopes of countering stereotypes and prejudice. And it does this, of course, through food. By giving Syrian refugees a way to introduce native Berliners to their homemade food through cooking classes, Über den Tellerrand makes it possible for people from different backgrounds and cultures to connect.

Of course, cities have long been cultural melting pots—with food both driving the cultural exchange and benefitting from it. Think of the *döner kebab*, which Turkish immigrants introduced to Germany in the 1950s and 1960s, or the huge range of cuisines from Asia, Africa, and the Americas you can find in cities such as London and New York. By welcoming refugees with open arms, projects such as Über den Tellerrand use the power of food to strengthen their communities and have a positive impact on society.

04

04 Über den Tellerrand offers Berliners cooking classes for Syrian, African, and Afghan cuisine.

05 Known as the "kitchen hub," Über den Tellerrand in Berlin brings people from all cultures together as they share their cooking experiences.

06 At The Blind Donkey in Tokyo, diners sit at a long table, facing the chefs as they work, striking a more intimate relationship between diners and chefs.

Then there are initiatives such as Eatwith.com, which also uses food to expand horizons. Founded in 2014 by Jean-Michel Petit and Camille Rumani, it's the world's largest community for authentic food experiences with locals. In essence, Eatwith.com is a web-based platform that allows people to "share unique dinners, cooking classes, food tours, and supper clubs with hand-selected hosts." Thanks to Eatwith.com, the adventurous traveler can now dine on a houseboat in Amsterdam, take a cooking class in Tokyo, or even eat an Italian feast with a family in Rome.

At the heart of the platform's success is its community—its global network of people who want to provide bona fide culinary experiences to travelers. After all, what is more authentic than discovering a local cuisine, with all its distinct customs and ingredients? And is there a more immersive, more intimate way to discover a new food culture than under someone's roof, at their own table? As the civil rights activist Cesar Chavez put it: "If you really want to make a friend, go to someone's house and eat with him … The people who give you their food give you their heart."

Food at Work

Faced with deadlines and other demands, many people struggle to sit down for a proper meal during the day at work. For some, lunch is a sandwich grabbed on the go. For others, it's a meal typically eaten *al desko*—hunched over the keyboard, staring at the screen. Which begs the question: if we don't eat with colleagues, what does that do to our workplace community?

That, at least, is the reason behind the growing popularity of canteens and cafeterias that provide communal meals for local workers or colleagues at the same company. Eschewing the bad old days of individuals eating lunch alone, the new generation of workplace canteens seek instead to encourage conversation and foster community spirit. Food is the social glue that forces workers to put down their tools, take a screen break, and take time to connect with one another.

Take, for example, Tuck Shop. Located in file-sharing giant Dropbox's Silicon Valley headquarters, it's a cafeteria that serves gourmet meals for breakfast, lunch, and dinner. Think: roasted lamb chops with butternut pumpkin purée, lavender-honey glaze, and lamb jus. Or, for dessert, a pumpkin *panna cotta* tart with cardamom whipped-cream, maple-poached cranberries, and candied pumpkin seeds. Everything is made from scratch: Tuck Shop grows its own microgreens, makes its own ice cream, and roasts its own coffee. For Dropbox employees, everything is free, of course. Predictably perhaps, corporate cafeterias are a common perk in Silicon Valley today. Employees at Bay Area start-ups Asana and Stripe have their own fancy canteens, too.

Then there's SOE (Studio Olafur Eliasson) Kitchen, which is housed in the Berlin studio of the acclaimed Icelandic-Danish artist Olafur Eliasson. The New York Times described it as "not quite a staff canteen and not quite an art studio." Indeed, it's where the studio's staff of 120 gathers four times a week for a communal lunch. A vegetarian meal is cooked by a kitchen team that includes Eliasson's sister, Victoria Elíasdóttir, who formerly worked at Dottir, a seafood restaurant in Berlin. A typical dish at SOE Kitchen might be garlic *shio-koji* tofu served with leek, chard, black radish, and miso-sesame sauce, or beet soup with horseradish crème fraîche. However, the point of the communal lunch isn't so much about delicious food as it is about providing inspiration: the meal often features a talk by a visiting

08

artist or scientist. Of course, it's also to build friendships and strengthen the collegial bonds between the staff at Eliasson's studio.

Then there are places such as Saltimporten Canteen, a restaurant located in a warehouse in the southern Swedish city of Malmö. It's only open for weekday lunch and it offers diners just two simple but wholesome dishes—lamb with tomatoes, nuts, and chili, say, or zucchini with lentils, raisins, and spinach. Moreover, Saltimporten Canteen operates as a de facto workplace cafeteria for the handful of companies that moved into the neighborhood in recent years. Pretty much everyone who leaves the office at lunchtime and grabs a seat at one of Saltimporten Canteen's long tables does so for the same reasons; for healthy and delicious food, of course, but also because they understand the value of sharing meals with others—with colleagues and locals. And the desire is the same: to build a community with people who were strangers until they sat down, and in the time-honored tradition, agreed to break bread with them.

07

07 Besides writing cookbooks to help fund its operation, Über den
    Tellerrand hosts special events, including a pop-up restaurant.

08 KitchenTown, an incubator for startups, has a café in which their
    makers can introduce their products to the local community.

09 Mil, in the Peruvian Andes, draws on the philosophy of indigenous
    farming communities and the ancient Incas.

09

SALA EQUIS

by Plantea

Having escaped the swing of the wrecking ball,
Sala Equis is a hip cultural venue in Madrid's happening
La Latina district.

Steeped in history, the Alba cinema first opened in the 1930s and has been
showing films on and off ever since (including a stint screening porno-
graphic movies in the 1980s). In a revamp orchestrated by a collaboration
between Plantea design studio and Payser Big & Small, the place has been
granted a new lease on life as a cool indie venue with a dedicated cultural
agenda. Seating a maximum of 55 people, the main auditorium is plush
and cozy. It runs a well-curated program of films at which guest directors,
actors, and writers offer Q&As. The true spirit of the place is captured
in the *plaza*, a fantastic indoor/outdoor space adorned with untreated walls,
peeling paint, and creeping foliage. The space features a large screen,
a bar, and seating that includes wooden benches, deck chairs, and swings.
With a finely curated line-up of films, concerts, and even the occasional
theater piece, Sala Equis draws a sophisticated local crowd.

Sala Equis dishes up a healthy selection of bar snacks, including a range of salads, burgers, and quiches.

Nothing feels too polished here. The original building has been preserved without too much renovation, and the new features are refreshingly rough and tumble.

SPIRITLAND

by Fraher Architects

A cool cultural hotspot since its extensive revitalization, London's Kings Cross is home to one of the city's hippest music venues.

Café by day and cocktail bar by night, Spiritland is also a respected fixture on London's vibrant music circuit. At the heart of its success lies originator Paul Noble's determination to offer "an opportunity to experience recorded music at an acoustic quality rarely heard in public." Having opened its doors in 2016, the venue seats 70 within a stylish interior packed with references to the music industry. The venue is also home to a radio production suite, Spiritland Sound Studio. Kitted out with a state-of-the-art, bespoke music system, and attracting a discerning crowd of dedicated followers, Spiritland runs a diverse program of music events seven days a week. Regular features include guest DJs and live performers, but talks and the occasional album launch also take place here.

THE BLIND DONKEY

In the heart of Tokyo's old town,
The Blind Donkey serves plates of Japan's finest,
freshest cuisine.

At The Blind Donkey, a long, wide counter runs the entire length of the restaurant. On one side, chefs busy themselves in the open kitchen, where the counter serves as their workspace. Surrounded by their ingredients, the cooks prepare each and every dish under the gaze of their patrons, who sit facing them on the opposite side of the counter. It's an arrangement that makes for a relaxed, convivial atmosphere. It's also an indication of the pride that the owners have in the food that they serve. This collaboration between chefs Jérôme Waag and Shin Harakawa pays homage to California's famed Chez Panisse, where Waag cooked for two decades. Here, as with Chez Panisse, the focus is on selecting ethically grown, environmentally sustainable produce that is organic and freshly harvested to create dishes that reflect the changing seasons.

The Blind Donkey takes its name from the life of Ikkyū, a legendary fifteenth-century Zen teacher.

Besides the
long dining
counter
opposite the
kitchen,
a few separate
tables stand
at the front of
the restaurant,
overlooking
the street.

(left) Chef Shin Harakawa prepares the fried potato dish
with aioli pictured above. Other bar snacks include
a carrot and daikon salad with *umeboshi*, or lettuce with
beets and herb cream.

LA RECYCLERIE

The "RE" of Parisian La REcyclerie
represents the restaurant's ethos to "reduce,
reuse, and recycle."

A stone's throw from the Porte de Saint-Ouen flea market at the city's northernmost limit, La REcyclerie is a collective effort that combines a restaurant, bar, café, farm, and vegetable garden in one location. This eco haven has a relaxed hippie vibe that sets the place apart from the sophisticated bistros more readily associated with the French capital. Housed in a railway station that's seen little locomotive activity since the Second World War, the main restaurant occupies a large hall with high ceilings, wrought-iron framework, and huge windows. True to its name, everything here is recycled, from the colorful lamps that hang above the bar to the jumble of chairs and tables that fill the space. The menu is based on what is available locally and set at budget prices, making this canteen-style dining at its best.

With a strong bias toward vegetarian dishes, all
of the food served at La REcyclerie is 100% homemade.

With the kitchen at one end and a bar running down the side,
the main dining hall has a relaxed, refectory vibe, with row upon
row of tables and chairs.

BENEDICT

There's only one thing you need to
know about Benedict and that is its motto:
"All About Breakfast."

At Benedict you really can order breakfast 24/7. The concept is the brainchild of Yair Kindler, who, along with his business partners Itay Pshigoda, Shay Kahana, and Guy Osadon, founded the first Benedict restaurant in Tel Aviv in 2006. In effortless, transnational style, theirs is a relaxed environment that blends the laidback ambience of Tel Aviv with New York slick and Euro bohemia. The breakfasts are scrumptious. You can order a classic German breakfast, a full English breakfast, New York Eggs Benedict (after which the place is named), a *croque madame* or a Middle Eastern *shakshuka*. There is also a whole host of dreamy pancakes, muesli, and fresh bagels. If anyone needs to know what time it is, the answer is always simple: it's breakfast time.

DISHES FILLED WITH LOVE

TOKYO, JAPAN

THE PASSION THAT FILLS THE DISHES AT TOKYO'S RESTAURANT EATRIP EXTENDS BEYOND THE PLATE AND INTO THE HEARTS OF THE DINERS

"Essentially, you have to eat to live, so what you choose to eat is very important." This seemingly simple mantra is key to restaurateur Yuri Nomura's venture, restaurant eatrip, in Japan's capital city. Wholesome, earthy, and largely organic, this restaurant is the manifestation of Nomura's personal exploration into the ways in which the food we eat and our everyday lives intersect one another. Crucial to her ethos is the idea that our meals should be as fresh and seasonal as possible, and, to this end, her team works closely with local farmers, bakers, and winemakers to assemble a menu that is as organic and close to nature as can be. It also follows that the less distance traveled, the more quality, freshness, and flavor are ensured.

Taking inspiration from the wisdom of generations long gone, Nomura also believes that the food we eat should be culturally sound. This idea is reflected in the restaurant's name. An amalgamation of the words "eat" and "trip," it represents the idea that eating here is a journey of some kind. With her dishes, Nomura hopes to awaken different feelings and senses in diners and to help them relate to past and future cultures through the food they eat. This leads seamlessly to another kind of fusion at play here—one that is seen in the menu. For while the ingredients are largely locally sourced and Japanese, the dishes on offer have a distinctly modern Mediterranean flair. Among the popular signature dishes are chicken-liver pâté and brandade of cod served with sourdough bread.

(right and below) Surrounded by flowers and the plants from the courtyard garden, it is easy to forget that this restaurant is in the heart of the city.

The food at eatrip changes with the seasons, but there is always a "Plate of Appetizers" on the menu.

TAKING INSPIRATION
FROM GENERATIONS
LONG GONE, NOMURA
BELIEVES THE FOOD
WE EAT SHOULD BE
CULTURALLY SOUND.

Meals are served simply but
beautifully, on wooden boards
and flat slate plates.

Open shelving and homemade desserts
contribute to the low-key, rustic
vibe of the place.

Nomura's desire to establish a deep-rooted connection between food and lifestyle comes to the fore in the restaurant itself. Located in the bustling Tokyo shopping district of Harajuku, the place is nevertheless tucked away in a backstreet. To access it, diners pass through a charming courtyard garden with a mossy stone path that leads through verdant shrubbery to the building's weathered wooden porch. Inside, Nomura has worked with designers from Tokyo-based interior design outfit Tripster to create a humble, rustic oasis in the city. She, herself, is acutely aware that this is an unusual and special location: "In this place, I can see not only the sky, but also the wind passing through the greenery. It was a miracle that I found this place."

Once inside, diners are enveloped in a tranquil simplicity that allows the food to take center stage. Beneath a blonde-wood ceiling crisscrossed with dark joists, the walls have been kept in their raw concrete finish or painted a sedate slate gray. Rustic tables and simply carved and upholstered wooden chairs stand on richly grained wooden floorboards. Bare light bulbs in the ceiling emit a warm glow. The all-important link between the kitchen and the diners is established here: waiters are slick and unobtrusive, serving beautifully arranged food on slate plates and wooden boards. The atmosphere is laid back, homey, and intimate. At the restaurant entrance and dotted among the tables are floral displays from the Little Shop of Flowers next door. Owned by Nomura's friend and

Over the years, Yuri Nomura has developed a close friendship with her florist neighbor, Iki Yukari.

NOMURA IS AWARE THAT THIS IS AN UNUSUAL AND SPECIAL LOCATION: "IT WAS A MIRACLE THAT I FOUND THIS PLACE."

Iki Yukari working
away in the Little
Shop of Flowers.
She also sells
gifts and household
items, such as
the apron worn by
Nomura.

collaborator, Iki Yukari, the store rein-
forces the emphasis on fresh,
natural, and organic produce that is
at the heart of this enterprise.

   Nomura's foray into the culinary
arena was not one of pure chance.
With a mother who teaches cooking
classes and a father who owns an
organic farm, the early influences in
her life are undeniable. Having studied
culinary arts in London and gone on
to work at Chez Panisse in Berkley,
California, Nomura is well-traveled
and in tune with Western cuisine.
With a genuine drive to instill her
passion for food in everyone, she
is—in addition to being a chef—
a self-made food director, writer,
and radio host. These days she entrusts
the cooking at restaurant eatrip
to a team headed by chef Takayuki
Shiraishi. With a kitchen that is
open to the restaurant, she hopes that
diners will get a sense of the love
that she and her team have for
working with high quality, fresh
ingredients that infuse the dishes.

With the Little Shop of Flowers as its backdrop,
the restaurant's terrace is swathed from above in
light-colored fabric, shading diners from the sun.

ONCE INSIDE, DINERS ARE ENVELOPED
IN A TRANQUIL SIMPLICITY THAT ALLOWS
THE FOOD TO TAKE CENTER STAGE.

Iki Yukari collaborates with Nomura on the
restaurant's plant and flower arrangements.

VOLLPENSION

With wholesome intentions and a huge dollop of fun, Vienna's Vollpension café is proof of that old saying that "grandma knows best."

What started as a social design initiative created for Vienna Design Week has grown over the past six years into the much-loved Vollpension café, located in the capital's Schleifmühlgasse. The simple premise is that no one cooks quite like grandma. Claiming (not without humor) to serve the best cakes and tarts in town, Vollpension also serves breakfast dishes and snacks with a strong emphasis on regional cuisine. The menu is rich in high-quality sausage, cheese, and bread-based snacks, which are served alongside hearty homemade lentil stew, potato salad, and goulash. And the granny element is no gimmick: all of the food is prepared and served by senior citizens — *Pensionäre* as they're called in German — hence the pun with "pension" in the café's name, which translates literally to "room and board."

PIADA

by Masquespacio

Aided by the Spanish creative consultancy
Masquespacio, siblings Mathilde and Arthur Plaza
realized their dream of transporting a little
piece of Italy to France.

The siblings' restaurant, Piada, lies in Lyon's Confluence
neighborhood, a city renowned for its diverse culinary culture.
Raised in France by Italian parents, their story is a touching
one: they took their mother's desire to bring her native *piadina*
to France, and they made it a reality. A popular street food, *piadine*
are a specialty of the Emilia-Romagna region—thin flatbreads
filled with Italian ham, cheese, and salad. Briefed to appeal to
a young clientele, Masquespacio's interior design reflects the
charm of 1950s Italian pop culture—fun, vibrant, and colorful.
Typical Italian features include the neon sign that reads "*un po di
Italianità*" ("A little Italian flair"), the mosaic tiles, lollipop globe
lamps, and arched structures that are reminiscent of traditional
Italian cafés. A distinctive Italian palette in yellows, blues,
purples, and pinks ties all the different design elements together.

MENUS

• **BUONO**　9,90
PIADINA OU SALADE +
BOISSON

• **BUONISSIMO**　12,50
PIADINA OU SALADE
+ BOISSON + DESSERT

**+1,50 POUR UNE BOISSON
PREMIUM***

**+2,50 POUR UN VERRE DE
VIN OU UNE BIÈRE
ARTISANALE**

• **BAMBINI**　6,50
UNE PIADINITA +UNE
BOISSON (EAU MINÉRALE,
SOFT OU JUS DE FRUITS)
+ UN DESSERT (SALADE DE
FRUITS OU COOKIE)

PIADINE

8,00

• **FAMOUSO** ROQUETTE, TOMATES SÉCHÉES,
HOUMOUS, GRAINES DE SÉSAME

• **MARE** SAUMON, CHICORÉE ROUGE,
RICOTTA, CIBOULETTE

• **RICETTA DEL CHEF** JAMBON
TRUFFÉ, SQUACQUERONE, ÉPINARDS,
ROQUETTE, TOMATES SÉCHÉES

• **GRANDE CLASSICO** PROSCIUTTO CRUDO
DI PARMA, SQUACQUERONE, ROQUETTE

• **BASILICO** PROSCIUTTO COTTO, TOMATES
CERISES, PARMIGIANO REGGIANO, PESTO

• **TOMOZZA** MOZZARELLA DI BUFALA,
TOMATE, BASILIC

• **SPECK'TACOLARIO** ÉPINARDS, CACIOTTA
AL PEPERONCINO, TABASCO, SPECK

*RECETTE IMAGINÉE PAR NOTRE PARRAIN C. PETEDOIE

INSAL

8,00

• **GRECA
ROMAGNOL**
TOMATE, CONCO
POIVRON, OIGN
ROUGE, PECORI
OLIVES KALAMA
BASILIC, ORIGAN
VINAIGRETTE AU
ROUGE

• **BUFALA**
MESCLUN, TOMAT
CERISES, MOZZA
DI BUFALA, VINAI
BALSAMIQUE, GR
DE SÉSAME

• **GAMBERETT**
ÉPINARDS, AVOCA
CAROTTE, CÉLERI
SAUCE AU CITRON
GRAINES DE COU
GRAINES DE TOUR

(top) Vittorio *piada* with guacamole, grilled bell peppers, pomegranate, red onion, and arugula; (below) Granata *piada* with red pesto, coppa, cherry tomatoes, and arugula.

Colorful tubes rise up the back wall. The lower tubes are soft cushion backs for the bench seats, while above they are plastic containers for plants.

UN PO DI ITALIANITÀ

The far wall of the restaurant is adorned with a graphic mosaic design in colors that match the colorful tubes.

RYÙ

by Menard Dworkind

The ancient Japanese tradition of *wabi sabi* plays a central role at restaurant Ryù in the Westmount neighborhood of Montreal.

Wabi sabi espouses the idea that beauty is enhanced by imperfection. Embracing this concept, Montreal-based interior designers at MRDK focused their contemporary design on natural and durable materials, like wood, that would take on a patina with age. There is a minimalist geometry at play here, reminiscent of traditional Japanese design, which is most evident in the light and dark wood slats above and the predominantly gray, black, and brown color scheme. It's a theme that is carried through to the presentation of the food—beautifully crafted sushi dishes served on black and white plates on bamboo mats. The circle, a feature of the Japanese flag, is a recurring motif. Above, suspended planters frame two large skylights, adding greenery and flooding the restaurant with natural light.

Wasabi root—a staple of Japanese cuisine—is often served grated. Eaten sparingly, it adds a hot and pungent flavor not dissimilar to horseradish.

Fresh fish features prominently on the menu at Ryù and includes wild striped bass, red snapper, tuna, and Japanese sea bream (pictured).

The Japanese influence is carried out to the last detail, from the bamboo
mats to the little ceramic dressing bowls and glazed clay pots.

With a double, full-height window frontage, Ryù has a strong presence from the street. A strict geometrical design ties in with the interior design.

LEGACY RECORDS
by Ken Fulk

Designed by the celebrated interior designer Ken Fulk, Legacy Records brings understated luxury to New York's rapidly expanding Hudson Yard district.

Housed in the former recording studio from which it takes its name, Legacy Records is the latest venture of Delicious Hospitality Group, aka Robert Bohr, Grant Reynolds, and chef Ryan Hardy, the team behind NYC's Charlie Bird and Pasquale Jones. Spanning over two stories, the enterprise features a fine-dining restaurant as well as a bar and café called Easy Victor. Known for his skill at layering textures and materials, Ken Fulk marries teak, marble, brass, grass cloth, and cane variously with emerald green in the restaurant and burnt orange in the bar and lounge. While the overriding vibe is one of smooth sophistication and elegance, soft-leather banquette seating introduces a relaxed comfort and intimacy throughout—elements that are frequently lacking in similar, somewhat formal settings.

There is no shortage of glitz at Legacy Records. Diners sit at leather-topped
tables, surrounded by rich wood cabinetry and brass fixtures and fittings.

MORE THAN JUST MACHINES

BALI, INDONESIA

L.A., USA

MILAN, ITALY

SYDNEY, AUSTRALIA

TOKYO, JAPAN

WITH CAFÉS IN FIVE
DIFFERENT PARTS
OF THE WORLD, FROM
TOKYO TO MILAN,
DEUS EX MACHINA
CONSIDERS ITSELF
MORE THAN A BRAND—
TODAY IT IS A
CULTURE, SPANNING
MOTORCYCLES, COFFEE,
FOOD, AND APPAREL

58

A fitting name, *Deus Ex Machina* translates as "god from the machine" in Latin. And while the core of this concept is indeed machines—customizing motorbikes was how everything started for founders Carby Tuckwell and Dare Jennings in Sydney in 2006—the brand has become far more than just motorbikes. In fact, Tuckwell describes his venture as more of a culture, with a strong emphasis on the community surrounding Deus Ex Machina and the cafés in particular: "People have developed friendships in our café based on their mutual love for all things Deus.... For our customers who were not familiar with Deus before coming into the café, they definitely feel the ethos of the brand during their first visit. Because so many of our regulars love the Deus brand, there is a sense of community," explained Carby.

Maintaining both a quality product and a quality experience lies at the heart of the Deus culture. This reflects what the founders describe as a "quality community." Valuing their customers and guests, Deus Ex Machina works hard at being inclusive of everyone as well as strengthening the community by hosting events in all their cafés. At the SuperOK event, everyone is invited for free food, drinks, and music on the last Friday of every month, and initiatives such as the "Bike Build Off" and "Surf Swap Meet" act as a celebration of all the guests' vehicles and surfboards, a large part of the Deus establishments.

Both Jennings and Tuckwell have a strong vision for their brand, which helps them stay true to the

61

"PEOPLE HAVE
DEVELOPED
FRIENDSHIPS IN
OUR CAFÉ BASED
ON THEIR MUTUAL
LOVE FOR ALL
THINGS DEUS."

A large billboard on the side of the
L.A. building offers inspiring quotes or
advertises the products on sale within.

Deus insignia and motorcycle-art
panels grace the exterior of
the flagship store in L.A.'s Venice
Boulevard.

initial spirit of the project despite
having ventured into many branches
of lifestyle—clothing, luggage,
bike accessories, books, prints, and
paintings are now for sale in eleven
Deus Ex Machina stores around
the world. In the cafés, guests enjoy
food, coffee, and cocktails in a
laid-back vibe, maintaining the original
vision and aesthetic; some would
call this "coolness" an integral part of
the Deus brand and culture. "We
like to think of Deus as a seed that
grows into a different tree depending
on the local soil it is planted in,
but they all ultimately share the same
roots," explains Tuckwell. And while
every café, whether in Canggu,
Bali, or Los Angeles, is slightly different with regard to the specific
menus and local specialties, you will
recognize many of the same details
in the different locations: the use of raw
concrete mixed with wood, the elegant
yet strong feel to the space, and
the overall style of the food. The menu
offers breakfast classics such as freshly
baked pastries and granola, while
for lunch, grilled panini sandwiches,
old-fashioned grilled cheese,
caprese salads, and the BLT are among
the time-tested classics on offer.

    The sourcing of local, organic
produce is another staple at Deus
cafés. At the Los Angeles outpost in
Venice, a local vendor, Farmers
Market Fairy, acts as a personal
farmers-market shopper with access
to high-quality produce sold at the
best markets in town. All produce
is hand-selected here, and when, for
instance, avocados are not in season in
late fall, avocado toast is taken off the

A barista pours a fresh coffee at the
Australian flagship store.

(Below and opposite) The Sydney flagship
store is situated in a 17,200-square-foot
(1,600-square-meter) renovated factory
building in Camperdown, Sydney.

TRULY LOYAL
CUSTOMERS RETURN
FOR THE COMMUNITY
SURROUNDING
THE DEUS CULTURE.

Poke bowls and salads are a
staple on the lunch and dinner
menus at the Sydney branch.

Besides coffee, the Sydney
café sells a wide range of
refreshing cocktails and
cold-pressed juice combos.

menu in the café. However, everything out of season is of course replaced with a delicious alternative—in this case Mediterranean toast consisting of ciabatta bread topped with hummus and marinated bell peppers, sprinkled with *herbes de Provence,* and drizzled with olive oil.

When in need of a quality cup of coffee, Deus Ex Machina café in Venice serves Vittoria Coffee, and the espressos are made from Vittoria's organic blend consisting of 100 percent Arabica beans. The way Tuckell sees it, people are impressed by the quality of the coffee, and this is what keeps them coming back. However, what the truly loyal customers, who make up a significant proportion of the clientele, really return for is the community surrounding the Deus culture. Permeating everything they do, whether it's opening up a new café or launching a new line of designer wear, the Deus philosophy of combining quality and coolness remains.

All of the Deus hallmark features can be found at the Milan outlet (below and opposite), as well as a courtyard extension of the café (bottom).

"WE LIKE TO THINK OF DEUS AS A SEED THAT GROWS INTO A DIFFERENT TREE DEPENDING ON THE LOCAL SOIL IT IS PLANTED IN."

WHAT WILL BE

ON OUR PLATES
TOMORROW?

How will we feed the planet's rapidly rising population? The alarming impact of the food industry on climate change demands new ideas. Alternative sources of protein, vertical farming, and the zero-waste movement all offer hope. Clearly there is no shortage of sustainable solutions—the only challenge now is to revolutionize our taste buds.

Lab-grown chicken. Bug burgers. Scrambled eggs made from plants. It might sound like science fiction, but these dishes are all destined to be on tomorrow's menu, alongside leafy greens grown in vast indoor farms. Why? Because by 2050, the world's population is expected to have topped 9 billion people, boosting the demand for food production by as much as 50 percent. And, as people in low- and middle-income countries get wealthier, they will crave more meat, fruit, and vegetables. The big question isn't how will we feed the planet, but how will we feed it *sustainably?*

The global food system *already* has a major impact on global warming, from the use of fossil fuels in fertilizers to deforestation to greenhouse gas emissions from livestock and transportation. "The way we produce food today is a massive driver of climate change," says Simon Caspersen, communications director at SPACE10, a Copenhagen-based research and design lab that's on a mission to design more sustainable ways of living. "It requires loads of resources for production, transport, and cooling; it uses our dwindling supplies of fresh water; and it's a major cause of deforestation."

Make no mistake: how we produce food has many consequences for people and the planet. For instance, conventionally grown crops may seem cheap—but the price we pay in shops tends not to cover the environmental cost of using harmful pesticides and herbicides. And, as the planet's population increases, the amount of arable land decreases, putting further pressure on the global food system. However, as the emergence of forward-thinking labs like SPACE10 suggests, the search is on for innovative solutions that can help feed our growing population sustainably.

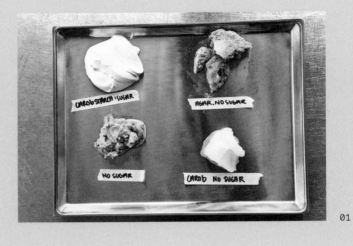

01

By 2050, the world's population is expected to have topped nine billion people, boosting the demand for food production by as much as 50 percent.

02

01   SPACE10 have turned their attention to making ice cream from hydroponically grown herbs and microgreens.

02   A pop-up farm by SPACE10, shows how crops can be grown hydroponically—that is, in nutrient-filled water rather than soil.

Down on the Farm

One much-trumpeted solution is vertical farming. Also known as indoor farming, it imagines a world where we can grow what we need, when we need it—without worrying about the weather. The world's largest vertical farm is operated in Newark, New Jersey, by AeroFarms. Thanks to the company's state-of-the-art aeroponic technology—which uses LED lights to mimic the sun and gives its crops the right mix of nutrients, water, and oxygen—AeroFarms produces locally grown, pesticide-free food, all year round, using 95 percent less water than conventionally grown food. Though the energy demands of vertical farms is high, when it comes to food miles, they couldn't be more local. Just look at the Good Bank, a restaurant in Berlin. It serves salads made with leafy greens grown in an indoor vertical farm located just behind the counter.

Then there's algae. Yes, algae—as in the green goo that clogs up waterways. Because it's packed with vitamins and minerals and and contains twice as much protein as meat does, algae has long been seen as a potential "super food." Today, it is being explored as an alternative to two ingredients partly responsible for the destruction of the rainforest— the soy protein that's used in animal feed; and palm oil, one of the key ingredients in many processed foods.

04

But nothing has grabbed the media's attention quite like the burgeoning food-tech movement. Take JUST, a San Francisco-based company that develops plant-based alternatives to popular dishes and ingredients—such as scrambled eggs made from mung beans. "We tap into the vast plant

03

As the emergence of forward-thinking labs like SPACE10 suggests, the search is on for innovative solutions that can help feed our growing population sustainably.

03 Spirulina is a strain of microalgae that looks set to play an increasing role in our diet of the future.

04 In a project dubbed "Tomorrow's Meatball," SPACE10 is looking at ways to create meatballs from alternative ingredients that include mealworms and root vegetables, such as carrots, parsnips, and beets.

kingdom to address what we believe is a limitation in the tools and mindset of the global food system," explains Andrew Noyes, head of communications at JUST.

JUST is also seeking to develop cultured Wagyu beef using cells from prized cows in Japan. That makes it one of several companies seeking to bring lab-grown meat to market and provide people with an alternative to meat produced from livestock. As well as allaying ethical concerns about eating meat, this would help reduce the greenhouse-gas emissions of the livestock industry.

Another way to do this, of course, is to use protein-packed insects in dishes—like the Bug Burger, a conceptual dish devised by SPACE10 and made with meal-worms, or the snacks made by companies such as Chirps Chips in California: made using cricket flour, they are a sustainable alternative to conventional wheat-based products.

06

05

The global food system *already* has a major impact on global warming, from the use of fossil fuels in fertilizers to deforestation to greenhouse gas emissions created by livestock and transportation.

05   SPACE10's Bug Burger is made from beet, parsnip, potato, and
      mealworm—the larval form of a darkling beetle.

06   Among the dishes on the Bad Taste menu is this salad of *hijiki*
      (a brown sea vegetable), cabbage, fried *mochi*, anchovy, sesame,
      bonito, and scallion.

The Way We Eat

07 A food technology room at JUST, Inc. Industrial kitchens of the future may look more like science laboratories than food plants.

08 At the QO in Amsterdam, over seventy varieties of vegetables, herbs, and fruit are grown in a greenhouse on the hotel's rooftop.

Though innovative solutions such as vertical farming will doubtless play an increasing role in the years to come, many people in the food industry believe we don't just need to change how we produce food, but what we eat too. Dan Barber is the founder of Blue Hill at Stone Barns, a restaurant north of New York City. His role as a chef, he says, is to influence the way people eat—and the agent of change is "deliciousness." From this perspective, restaurants such as Blue Hill should be seen as "cathedrals of ideas" that can help change food culture. For example, when chefs champion legumes like lentils and chickpeas, those ingredients are more likely to "trickle down" into the mainstream. Barber has cited the popularity of Greek yogurt and quinoa as proof of the influence of restaurants on consumer taste.

07

Others see art as a vehicle for changing how people think about food and how to consume it. Take Jen Monroe, who runs a project in Brooklyn called Bad Taste. She throws creative dinners featuring "edible artworks" that advocate using seafood ingredients like octopus and seaweed rather than overstocked fish such as tuna and salmon. "Depicting what our diets could, by necessity, look like in 30 years as a result of the loss of certain familiar food sources is a clear way to make some of these changes less abstract," she explains.

08

Learning From Nature

Then there's the burgeoning ze-ro-waste movement, whose propo-nents seek to make better use of the food they've already got—often by redefining what should be considered "waste." Take the Copenhagen-based restaurant Amass, founded by former Noma head chef Matt Orlando. It is pioneering a closed-loop system in which everything it produces is reused, if possible. At Amass, for example, any leftover table water is collected at the end of the night, sterilized, and used for cleaning and in the aquaponic system, while used coffee grounds are baked into cookies.

Ultimately, of course, reducing waste and food miles is about reconnecting with the land and redefining the value of food. "Human beings have had only the blink of an evolutionary eye to invent things, while nature has benefited from a 3.8-billion-year head start in research and develop-ment," explains Caspersen. "With that level of investment, it only makes sense to look to nature for solutions before trying to invent them ourselves. We need to be better at learning from nature and working with it."

To that end, education will surely be key—especially our children's. Activist Alice Waters helped pio-neer the farm-to-table movement in the 1970s when she opened her restaurant Chez Panisse in Berkeley, California. In 1995 she launched the Edible Schoolyard Project at a school nearby. Its hope was that by showing children how to maintain a garden, they would understand as young as possible where their food comes from—and thus become ambas-sadors for future generations.

Ultimately, reducing waste and food miles is about reconnecting oneself to the land and redefining the value of food.

As we seek more sustainable means of producing food, it's clear that there's no silver bullet, no one-size-fits-all solution. Organic farming and the pursuit of deli-ciousness will surely sit alongside innovative ideas such as lab-grown meat and cricket flour. And ac-cording to Caspersen, emerging technologies such as AI and block-chain could also help "increase efficiency, transparency, traceabil-ity, food safety, and collaboration throughout the food system."

Yet no matter what combination of solutions we embrace, one thing is clear: the choice to sup-port a more environmentally friendly food system is certainly ours as consumers and diners to make. Indeed, as Alice Waters put it in her 2017 memoir, *Coming to My Senses: The Making of a Counterculture Cook,* "Eating is an everyday experience, and the decisions we make about what we eat have daily consequences. And those daily consequences can change the world."

09 Preparation for lunch at SPACE10. Whatever's on the menu,
it's likely that any herbs, leaves, and vegetables will have been
grown hydroponically.

CASAPLATA

by Lucas y Hernández-Gil

With a purposefully neutral interior, Seville's Casaplata seeks to "blur the lines of the environment to focus on what is within reach."

While it is the norm for modern restaurants to impress customers with their designer interiors, Casaplata has taken the opposite approach. In a bid to center customers' attention on their fine Mediterranean cuisine, the restaurateurs have opted for a sleek, silver-gray, almost industrial backdrop. That's not to say the interior is without interest. Created by Milan-based Lucas y Hernández-Gil architect studio, the rooms are subtle in their decoration. A circular motif runs throughout the design and a private dining area has a hint of pink. Inspired in part by Giorgio Morandi's works—still lifes in soft and muted neutral tones— the architects have chosen furnishings in pastel hues to add accents of color. The effect is striking and brings a breath of fresh air to a city where there is a penchant for a more nostalgic, historical-revival approach to interior design.

The circular theme can be seen throughout the interior design—in wall mirrors, lighting, tables, and a circular opening between the bar area and dining room.

NAIM

by the Stella Collective

Beyond the jade-green arch that frames the café entrance, Naim presents a Middle-Eastern oasis in the heart of Brisbane.

The jade green continues within, on the floor tiles that line the café. They complement the soft rose-pink tones of the tables and chairs and the brass fittings and fixtures beyond. This is the work of Hana Hakim of the Stella Collective. Sharing a Syrian heritage with the café owners, Hakim has created a modern take on Islamic architecture and, specifically, the internal courtyard. All the familiar elements are here, delivered with a twist that is Hakim's own. Rattan backrests and a brass screen above the water fountain evoke the traditional *mashrabiya* screens that filter light through windows. The textured gray walls are offset by pristine white tiling featuring a geometric design that reinterprets the ancient Arabic art. Framed in black steel, the room is bordered by deep-green foliage—a finishing touch for what Hakim describes as her "bountiful oasis."

PERSIJN RESTAURANT AND JUNIPER & KIN

by TANK

QO Hotel's Persijn Restaurant has an open-plan kitchen and centrally located bar that create a sense of openness and symbolize the transparency of the place.

Restaurant Persijn, located in QO Hotel in Amsterdam—a city hotel with a sustainable approach to traveling and accommodation—was designed by Amsterdam-based architectural studio TANK. The ground-floor restaurant features two glass staircases and a voluminous timber-slated bar that subdivides two seating areas. One of these areas is extravagantly decorated with pale green and pink velvet chairs, plush sofas, and brass pendant lights, while the other has a patterned black-and-white tiled floor, olive green seating, and warm wooden tables. Round concrete columns and heavy concrete pilasters contrast with the luxurious upholstery, lend the space a raw edge. Over 70 varieties of vegetables, herbs, and fruit grow in the rooftop greenhouse and pools with fish provide fresh ingredients for the restaurant kitchen, allowing the restaurant to operate as sustainably as possible.

A botanical theme runs throughout
the hotel. The plant inside
this Pikaplant Jar continuously
recycles the water it has, so it
never needs watering.

Juniper & Kin is a seductive bar on the 21st floor of Amsterdam's OO building. With its dark, low-lit interiors, it serves cocktails that are works of art in their own right (opposite).

The dishes served at Persijn are exquisitely presented, with the ingredients in their purest state and featuring plants grown in the rooftop greenhouse.

TACOFINO OASIS

by Shiloh Sukkau

With a nod to the mid-century "Acapulco look," the latest incarnation of the Tacofino brand lightens the mood in Vancouver's financial district.

With a string of outlets in Vancouver, Canada, Tacofino is a hit with locals. The food is West Coast inspired with an emphasis on burritos, nachos, and tacos. According to its owners, Tacofino Oasis really is just that—"an oasis in the concrete towers of the surrounding financial district." The interior, designed by Shiloh Sukkau, takes inspiration from the "Acapulco look" pioneered by Mexican interior designer Arturo Pani. Lined with wicker stools, a zany terrazzo bar zigzags through the restaurant—a clever device for separating the dining area from the kitchen. In the main seating area, customers sit on stools at handmade tables made from pink cement, or along a wooden banquette with striped upholstery. Above the tables, skylights fill the space with light. The dominant color is a cheery red, set against the turquoise walls and ceiling.

The main restaurant area is flooded with natural light from solarium-style skylights above.

In a novel touch, the menu is printed in white on wood-veneer panels fixed to a grill at the far end of the dining room.

The main room extends out onto a large patio via ceiling-height sliding glass doors.
The patio is furnished with bubblegum-pink wire-mesh chairs.

KITCHENTOWN:

BRINGING INNOVATION TO THE WORLD OF FOOD

HAILING FROM SILICON VALLEY, RUSTY SCHWARTZ CREATED AN INCUBATOR FOR FOOD START-UPS TO SUPPORT A BUZZING NEW FOOD TECH SCENE

SAN FRANCISCO
BAY AREA, USA   91

Imagine if the innovation, productive mindsets, and resources of the tech industry in Silicon Valley were applied to advanced food concepts. Rusty Schwartz, a self-proclaimed "tech guy," questioned why so few resources were invested in supporting food start-ups compared to the tech industry. He saw the need for an incubator that focuses solely on food start-ups, helping them create and scale in the smartest way possible; Schwartz founded KitchenTown to fill this gap.

KitchenTown is located in San Mateo, part of an area known to locals as the Peninsula just north of Silicon Valley in California, in a shared 20,000-square-foot (1,860-square-meter), multi-use warehouse and production facility. Here, Schwartz and his team have helped pave the way for more than 400 start-up businesses in the food industry since 2014, and today the space includes both a café and a restaurant besides the facilities designed to mentor, support, and foster food start-ups. As Schwartz explains in an earlier interview, he wasn't the first to create a food incubator, but the few that previously existed didn't have the capacity to accommodate bigger projects and larger-scale facilities. As KitchenTown helps start-ups grow, it, too, has been scaling up. Their second location is a large warehouse in San Francisco and they now intend to expand to Berlin.

Together with his partner Alberto Solis, Schwartz founded KitchenTown as he was certain of the vital role an incubator can play in the crucial first year of a company. At this point, many founders are looking for guidance and a better understanding of potential pitfalls. KitchenTown provides advice on everything from legal questions to ingredient sourcing, as well as offering a large production space that not many companies starting out can afford on their own. Food entrepreneurs can bring their team to the KitchenTown facilities and start producing at a larger scale. From education, peer-learning opportunities, product development, to distribution, KitchenTown helps level the playing field for early-stage ventures in an industry that is both complex, fiercely competitive, and unforgiving.

To date, KitchenTown has created more than 300 jobs and raised more than $50 million (€44 million) in funding. Working with a select group of start-ups, KitchenTown puts a special emphasis on the environmental approach of possible entrepreneurs: "When it comes to food, better, more nourishing, diverse foods is a primary filter. Clean label is table stakes. And so is sustainability. From crops and ingredients that are used and care for workers throughout the value chain, to the type of packaging and overall environmental sustainability, our founders have to be aware how they and their products measure up," explains Schwartz. Thus, working for a better tomorrow for our planet is the common denominator of every project KitchenTown is involved with. One of these is ReGrained, a company that has found a way to make use of the spent grain from beer production, turning these into energy bars. Creating their product with the key notion of "edible upcycling,"

The distinctive frontage of KitchenTown's 20,000-square-foot (1,860-square-meter) building. The company logo echoes the shape.

KITCHENTOWN HELPS LEVEL THE PLAYING FIELD FOR EARLY STAGE VENTURES IN AN INDUSTRY THAT IS BOTH COMPLEX, FIERCELY COMPETITIVE, AND UNFORGIVING.

The enterprise includes a large kitchen area fitted with all the necessary equipment for scaling up a start-up food operation.

ReGrained sees opportunities in the use of leftovers from the food industry, and works for a better alignment of the food we eat with the planet we love. The ReGrained founders still remember their humble beginnings: "We started as one of your smallest makers using the commercial kitchen space. It was a huge upgrade from the dilapidated kitchen we were in before! We were still working on the business part time and really just getting going. Since then, the relationship has really deepened in an incredible way." Today, the shift from small start-ups to successful businesses is evident: ReGrained was given the opportunity to set up a partnership and receive investment from Barilla, thanks to KitchenTown who introduced the entrepreneurs to the pasta giant.

Providing a network to the start-ups involved is one thing, but KitchenTown is also able to assist a start-up company in kicking off and taking their production to the next level. Siren Snacks, a company that creates protein snacks from vegan plant protein, is proof of this. With the help of KitchenTown, they evolved from the final recipe development of their protein bar to having stores and orders lined up. Siren Snacks founders describe KitchenTown as "the perfect ecosystem for small food companies to thrive," where both the staff in the production kitchen and the group of promising companies working in the same space inspire one another and help each other grow.

For Beau Perry, founder of seaweed farming company Blue Evolution, connecting with KitchenTown has been a great resource in broadening his network and gaining substantial insights that he feels he would not have had the advantage of otherwise. With his company, Perry sustainably sources seaweed from North America and turns it into delicacies such as penne or rotini pasta infused with seaweed. Visiting different food business and hearing from industry experts has helped Blue Evolution build a better-informed approach to offering their seaweed-based pasta to end-consumers.

As Perry explains, "Rusty had done a great job of identifying an acute need among sustainable food start-ups for various forms of support through the gauntlet of launching a brand into this very complicated and competitive space. We're dealing with challenges that we share with so many other great companies trying to change the world through food, and the prospect of us each going it alone is fraught and perilous."

Whether it's providing a network of start-ups and high-profile investors or offering entrepreneurial facilities from where they can kick off their dream food company, Schwartz has brought innovation, resources, and productivity to the industry. In the midst of expanding to Berlin, Schwartz believes that growth comes from the people you surround yourself with, and from partnering with others who believe in what you are doing. KitchenTown has put these words into effect for a large number of start-ups already, with even more planned for the future.

Blue Evolution grows its own seaweed in onshore and offshore farms in Mexico and Alaska.

WORKING FOR A BETTER TOMORROW FOR OUR
PLANET IS THE COMMON DENOMINATOR OF ALL
PROJECTS KITCHENTOWN IS INVOLVED WITH.

Taking spent grain from the beer-brewing process, ReGrained makes a flour that is used to make their wholesome, high-energy food bars.

PROSSIMA FERMATA

by Studio Wok

Highly polished surfaces and clever graphics
set the scene for this laboratory-style ice cream
parlor in Milan.

This unique *gelateria* is the creation of Studio Wok, and it perfectly embodies their concept of the owner as master craftsman in need of a state-of-the-art artisanal workshop. Since they were working with limited space, the team wanted the ice cream to be made and sold in a single, unified space. A gleaming, industrial-looking counter takes center stage. Beneath it, a plum-colored linoleum floor echoes the color of the packaging. Toward the back of the store, two refrigerators stand in a custom-built wooden frame and display fresh and seasonal fruits grouped by color. The separate elements are well integrated through the clever combination of industrial and natural materials, and they conjure a clean, friendly vibe. To complete the laboratory theme, the wall opposite the counter features graphics by the design studio Atto—images of the sweet treats on offer.

POKE POKE

by Studio Doho

Creatives at Studio Doho coined the term "urban surf" to describe their design for this Hawaiian poke bowl concept in Shanghai.

While designing this fun fast-food outlet, the creative duo Xin Dogterom and Jason Holland faced a number of limitations from the start. Not only was the space small at 340 square feet (32 square meter), but its facade was little more than a solid concrete wall. In addressing the size issue, Studio Doho crafted an exterior counter that curves into the interior ordering area, linking the outside and inside space to optimize seating for customers. To alter the facade, the designers framed the door and windows in bold red and covered the huge expanse of bare wall with a striking mosaic — a graphic representation of the ocean where the water meets the sky. Other maritime motifs include a wavy counter, fish-inspired artwork inside the restaurant, and surfboard-shaped bar counters on the facade. Attracting curious passersby, Poke Poke is a triumph of urban design.

Hawaiian-style poke bowls are the mainstay of the menu,
made to order with the freshest ingredients.

The undulating serving counter doubles as a chiller
cabinet for the poke bowl ingredients.

Small tables and bench seating help to maximize space in
the compact eating area.

An innovative
design allows
the storefront
to function
as a service
window for the
outdoor seating
area.

EGG KNEIPE

The brainchild of three egg fanatics, Berlin's
Egg Kneipe on Kottbusser Damm has made this farm
staple the star of the show.

The humble egg is one of the world's simplest foods, but it is
also one of the most versatile. It was this seemingly contra-
dictory statement that led Daniel Günther, Patrick Walter, and
Thies Wulf to believe there might be something in running
an "egg bistro." And they were right. Since opening its doors in
2017, the Egg Kneipe already has a growing number of fans,
or "eggsters" as the trio like to call them, who keep coming back
for more. Regulars on the menu include egg rolls, egg sandwiches, and omelets, and served alongside burgers, salads, and
protein bowls. The quirky interior design includes a half-wood,
half-metal bar with welded details, a smattering of barstools,
and three original ship's portholes separating the dining area from
the kitchen. The guys describe the look as "steampunk nautico."

A "Fitness"
egg roll,
filled with
spinach,
cottage
cheese, dried
tomato,
fried egg,
carrot,
and cucumber.

The owners have a collection of egg
memorabilia that is growing steadily, thanks
to donations from fans of the bistro.

The "steampunk nautico" look, with ship's lanterns set into the metal framework of the bar as well as a wall of glazed green tiles.

PINK ZEBRA

by Renesa Studio

In the words of the creative minds behind this project, "How about we dip a zebra into a deep pink sea?"

With its bizarre design, the Pink Zebra, aka the Feast India Co., is at once glamorous, surreal, and mesmerizing. Occupying two stories of a colonial building in the Indian city of Kanpur, the establishment features a dining area downstairs, a lounge/bar upstairs, and a covered terrace. Pink Zebra is awash with color inside and out; the building is also emblazoned with bold black-and-white stripes. Taking cues from the aesthetic of filmmaker Wes Anderson, the effect is a mix of European colonial grandeur with a dash of Art Deco and Indian kitsch. Charged with creating this visual treat, creatives Sanchit Arora and Sanjay Arora of Renesa Architecture Design Interiors have fulfilled their desire to create spaces that are a "hybrid rather than pure—compromising rather than clean," and which "leave the visitor hanging in the middle of an artistic sea."

The Pink Zebra makes for a surreal vision on the streets of Kanpur: the pink walls and zebra stripes contrast with the colonial style architecture.

Upstairs, the slatted pergola roof is open to the elements, enhancing the striped effect, casting strips of light and shadow across the terrace.

At the Pink Zebra, even the furniture, light fixtures, and accents have the same pink hue.

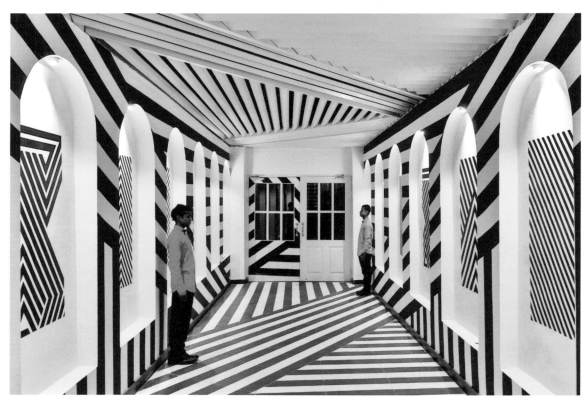

Strolling the corridors of the building can be a disorienting experience, the black and pink stripes adding a psychedelic effect.

ATOBOY

With a "shareable tasting menu of small plates,"
New York's Atoboy offers a dining experience where
the side dishes take center stage.

Atoboy is a canteen-style restaurant on East 28th Street in
New York's NoMad district. Diners sit at two rows of wooden
tables between raw concrete walls. The byline on the menu
reads "Korean-Inspired Small Plates," and the attraction here
is just that—chef-owner Junghyun Park's personal interpretation
of *banchan*, a staple of Korean cuisine. With a repertoire that
changes seasonally, Atoboy typically offers 18 small dishes
from which each guest is encouraged to choose three. The range
of vegetable, fish, and meat platters features Korean favorites
such as lotus root, pork belly, and sea urchin—all served with
rice and homemade kimchi. The food arrives in stages, and the
plates get passed around before piling up, empty, at the center
of the table. This is convivial eating at its best.

DOOT DOOT DOOT & FLAGGERDOOT
by Carr

Carr architects reinvent the "destination hotel,"
raising the bar to a whole new level of sophistication.

Surrounded by the stunning vineyards of Australia's Mornington Peninsula,
the Jackalope Hotel has a history of winemaking. This viticulture is the
inspiration for Carr architects' mesmerizing interiors. Designed to capture
the wonders of alchemy and the transformative process of distillation,
the hotel is a fusion of curious objects, furniture, and installations, specially
commissioned to create a unique experience for guests. Edgy installations
and a bespoke electric-blue pool table give the cocktail bar Flaggerdoot its
cool vibe while, in the restaurant Doot Doot Doot, an awesome 10,000-bulb
installation by Fabio Ongarato Design undulates across the ceiling. In a
bold move, the overwhelmingly dominant color throughout the hotel complex
is black, lifted by accents of gold, silver, copper, and bronze.

A mysterious, dark glamor has been meticulously curated in both the Doot Doot Doot restaurant (opposite) and the Flaggerdoot bar (below).

In keeping with the interior design of the place, the food is stylishly presented on black crockery.

BIG,
BIGGER,
BIGGEST

PARIS,
FRANCE

FOCUSING ON THE
SIMPLE THINGS IN
LIFE, BIG MAMMA
SERVES UP GENEROUS
HELPINGS OF TOP-
QUALITY ITALIAN
CUISINE

The Big Mamma enterprise has taken Paris by storm in recent years with its range of Italian cocktail bars and restaurants, which includes Popolare, East Mamma, Pink Mamma, and Mamma Primi. Thinking "big" in name alone has seen co-founders Tigrane Seydoux and Victor Lugger develop a winning formula that has customers coming back in droves. This duo has opened no fewer than eight venues since first launching in 2015. They are also proud to have created the largest restaurant in Europe, La Felicità. The secret of their success lies in the co-founders' unwavering dedication to offering "an authentic Italian cuisine, at the best price, served by a young and friendly Italian team." Their recipe for success is as simple as that.

   The Big Mamma story extends back further than the establishment of the group's first restaurant, though: the idea grew from the seeds that were planted in Tigrane Seydoux and Victor Lugger's childhood memories of family vacations to Italy. It was on these trips that, as boys, the two of them developed the deep-rooted passion for Italian food that drew them together as business partners. Each of them was struck by the ease and comfort with which you could eat simply and cheaply in the popular trattorias that are so much a part of Italian cuisine. Sharing the same vision, they sought to recreate a convivial, fuss-free atmosphere in restaurants of their own. With Italian food an all-time favorite across the globe, they had a ready-made market for their enterprise;

On the menu at Pink Mamma is *the burrata crémeuse*, a mozzarella dish served with olives and tarragon or sun-dried tomatoes.

The founders of the Big Mamma Group: Tigrane Seydoux (left) and Victor Lugger (right).

"ITALIAN CUISINE IS SYNONYMOUS WITH GENEROSITY, A VISION OF GASTRONOMY THAT WE STRONGLY APPROVE OF AND WANT TO SHARE WITH PEOPLE."

(left and above) The four-story Pink Mamma restaurant in the 9th arrondisement. Each floor has a different interior design.

A typical Big Mamma restaurant menu, featuring pasta and pizza dishes as well as a number of regional specialties.

the challenge was how to stand out. In their ambition to set themselves apart from other Italian restaurants, Seydoux and Lugger traveled widely throughout Italy before embarking on their business. Their mission: to find local producers with whom they could forge lasting relationships. The quality of the food is paramount, but the simplicity of the dishes and the generosity with which they are served is also key, and traditional dishes such as San Daniele ham, pizza margherita, truffle pasta, and tiramisu are staples. In seeking to recreate the authentic trattoria vibe, the firm enlisted the services of star designer Martin Brudnizki, "a real visionary [who] knows perfectly how to create spaces with a strong design, whilst keeping the warmth and welcoming feel of each." Such is his skill, that Brudnizki blends high-quality materials with rough and rustic finishes to add a touch of originality to each space. Each restaurant has its own distinct interior design, while sharing commons themes, such as the brightly colored, hand-painted Italian ceramics that many of the dishes are served on. Finally, comes the conviviality. With a predominantly Italian staff, Big Mamma hopes "to create cozy and warm trattorias, where our clients feel comfortable and want to stay for hours to eat, drink, and chat." The overriding feeling is one of great warmth for the customers and a passionate pride in the food being served.

Perhaps the most ambitious venture to date, La Felicità is a single, enormous space inside Halle Freyssinet at Station F in Paris's

Chefs prepare food in the open kitchen at Mamma Primi in the Batignolles neighborhood of Paris.

Profiterole Napolitaine, served at Big Mamma's Pizzeria Popolare. This tempting dessert is served with a delicious hot chocolate sauce.

BRUDNIZKI BLENDS
HIGH-QUALITY
MATERIALS WITH
ROUGH AND RUSTIC
FINISHES TO
ADD A TOUCH OF
ORIGINALITY
TO EACH SPACE.

up-and-coming 13th arrondisement. Despite the fully grown trees and train carriages, you wouldn't guess the venue covered around 43,055 square feet (4,000 square meters) of indoor and outdoor space in total. The interior design is incredibly smart: the development is divided into sections housing a food market, several separate eateries, a beer garden, and an impressive cocktail bar, all emanating the same Italian vibe.

When you enter a Big Mamma restaurant, the smells, sights, and sounds immediately transport you to Italy. Essentially, it is this that lies behind the success of the brand and is the culmination of Seydoux and Lugger's Italian dream: "Italian cuisine is synonymous with generosity, a vision of gastronomy that we strongly approve of and want to share with people. We wanted to bring everything back to Paris—not only the produce and food, but also the atmosphere, the warmth, and the people."

Authentically rustic-looking pizzas are served at the pizzeria of La Felicità.

THE OVERRIDING FEELING IS ONE OF GREAT WARMTH FOR THE CUSTOMERS AND A PASSIONATE PRIDE IN THE FOOD BEING SERVED.

The enormous trattoria at La Felicità, complete with railway carriage.

CELEBRATING

CULINARY
TRADITIONS

Portuguese bakery Pastéis de Belém is preserving decades-old pastry recipes to great success in Lisbon, and the chef at St. John restaurant in London is reclaiming the long-forgotten "nose-to-tail" tradition—and has earned a Michelin star in the process. It's clear that embracing one's cultural and culinary heritage to create a unique sense of place is an essential ingredient for success in today's competitive food scene.

A food culture is made up of many things: its people and customs; its recipes and ingredients; its history and traditions. These elements often combine in the most alluring way. Think of a traditional market street such as Rue Mouffetard in Paris, or London's Portobello Road. It's still common to see locals buying fresh ingredients at market stalls or popping in and out of traditional butchers, bakeries, and fishmongers, their shopping bags bursting with groceries. The unique sense of place is unmistakable—and utterly intoxicating. It's a lesson that many establishments are increasingly adopting. To stand out from the crowd and keep attracting patrons, many bars, bakeries, cafés, and restaurants are proudly celebrating their traditions and heritage—ensuring that their history is central to the story they tell.

At Pastéis de Belém, a picturesque bakery just outside Lisbon, visitors are struck by the intricately tiled walls and the intoxicating smell of fresh *pastéis de nata,* or egg custard tarts. The bakery's story dates to 1837, when a local monastery sold it the tart recipe.

Back then, the monks used egg whites to starch their clothes— and with no use for the yolks, they developed a recipe for what is now known worldwide as the quintessential Portuguese treat. Not that other cafés haven't tried to replicate them. But they'll never taste as good as the ones at Pastéis de Belém, where customers can look through the window and watch them being made by hand. "Tradition will always live in a modern context, and in this case, tradition and history are what define this house and brand," says Miguel Clarinha, manager of Pastéis de Belém.

With centuries of history, traditional places have been tried and tested over time, preserving local customs and cultural knowledge for generations to come. Dating back to 1621, Zur letzten Instanz is the oldest pub in Berlin. In its dark, paneled rooms, diners can enjoy typical Berlin dishes such as *Eisbein* (ham hock) and *Kohlroulade* (cabbage roulade).

02

To stand out from the crowd, manybars, bakeries, cafés, and restaurants are proudly celebrating their traditions and heritage—ensuring that their history is central to the story they tell.

Having changed hands many times, Zur letzten Instanz has been owned by the Sperling family since 1980. "I helped here as a small child," says restaurant manager Anja Sperling. "It is like a second home for me."

Schwartz's Deli in Montreal dates back to 1928 and is often described as "the oldest deli in Canada." Founded by Reuben Schwartz, the Montreal institution is now owned by the Nakis and Angélil-Dion families—two families of restaurateurs who joined forces so that locals could keep eating its juicy meat sandwiches.

01

01   Now familiar worldwide, the bite-size egg-custard pastries known in Portugal as *pastéis de nata*.

02   Berlin's Zur letzten Instanz in days gone by. Even Napoleon is rumored to have been served here.

The deli's signature dish is a rye-bread sandwich filled with smoked meat and a generous dollop of mustard. Cured for 10 days, with a strong flavor and a soft texture, it's a must-have for tourists and locals alike.

Similarly, no visit to Vienna is complete without a slice of *sachertorte*, the Austrian layered chocolate cake. It has long been disputed whether the original recipe came from the Demel bakery or the Sacher Hotel—two establishments whose heritage goes back centuries. Either way, *sachertorte* has not lost its appeal. For some, it brings back childhood memories. For others, it is the best way to discover that unique sense of place that defines the Austrian capital.

03

"Nose-to-tail eating is common sense. Tripe and onions soothes you as well as lifts your spirit. Not a lot of food can do both at the same time." Fergus Henderson, co-owner of St. John restaurant.

04

03 At Fotografiska in Stockholm, guests are encouraged to choose from a menu of seasonal vegetable dishes with meat or fish as a side dish.

04 St. John restaurant in Clerkenwell, London with its stripped-back whitewashed walls. It has an in-house bakery producing traditional puddings and bread loaves.

Looking for Inspiration in the Past

Then there's the Argentinean restaurant Anahi in Paris— a favorite with design devotees and meat lovers alike. Architects transformed a traditional French butcher's shop into an elegant dining room. By preserving the space's original structure and tiled walls, the restaurant celebrates the long history of small groceries in Paris while creating a vision for the future of the space.

Ateljé Finne, in Helsinki, demonstrates another successful transformation of a space that spans time and tradition. What used to be sculptor Gunnar Finne's studio has been turned into a restaurant that looks like a minimalist art gallery.

Chefs are starting to explore the culinary culture of a place, seeking out everything from traditional recipes for local dishes and historical methods such as fermentation and preservation, to cherished eating rituals and neglected ingredients.

In fact, Finne designed the studio himself, and his realistic sculptures, made between 1886 and 1952, are displayed amid whitewashed brick walls. The restaurant serves typically New Nordic cuisine, like Baltic herring confit and deer heart medallions finished off by lingonberry mousse.

05

05 The Lina Stores restaurant in London's Soho continues a long tradition of Italian food in the heart of the city, which started with a delicatessen of the same name in the 1940s.

06 Fergus Henderson of St. John restaurant in Clerkenwell, London. He established the eatery with partner Terry Gulliver in 1994—early pioneers of the modern British food movement.

When Old Meets New

In today's increasingly globalized world, thanks to mass production, mass agriculture, and mass consumption, tradition can sometimes be lost—and, with it, that unique sense of place. In response, some chefs are starting to explore their roots or the particular culinary culture of a place, seeking out everything from traditional recipes for local dishes and historical methods such as fermentation and preservation, to cherished eating rituals and neglected or little-used ingredients. Doing so gives them a chance to create something they can call their own, something that reflects their identity, something unique.

A pioneer of the "nose-to-tail" movement, which creatively uses every part of the animal, is chef Fergus Henderson, founder of the Michelin-starred restaurant St. John in London. "Once you knock the animal on the head, it seems right to enjoy all the things that lie beyond the fillets," says Henderson. If you've ever wondered what trotters, tripe, or chitterlings taste like, St. John is the place to go. Henderson puts a modern spin on traditional British cuisine with dishes like braised duck leg with carrots and aioli, and roast wigeon with braised red cabbage. "Nose-to-tail eating is common sense," he explains. "Tripe and onions soothes you as well as lifts your spirit. Not a lot of food can do both at the same time."

For today's forward-thinking chefs, the most important task is to keep traditions alive while also running a sustainable kitchen. If they continue to source inspiration from both the past and the future, we can all look forward to many more ambitious restaurants and cuisines.

07

St. John's success not only is an example of how an age-old craft can become a modern restaurant concept, it also shows the enormous positive influence that chefs that can have. And from fine-dining establishments such as Dan Barber's restaurant Blue Hill to more casual joints like Kumpel & Keule— a butcher's shop in Berlin that makes burgers with trimmings from their dry-aged beef— increasing numbers of restaurants have a similar zero-waste philosophy and showcase ingredients that would normally be thrown away.

Michelin-starred restaurant Bo.lan in Bangkok is celebrating the country's food culture by embracing long-forgotten dishes and traditions. "We believe in showcasing and supporting the biodiversity of Thai produce as well as safeguarding Thai food

Increasing numbers of restaurants have a similar zero-waste philosophy and showcase ingredients that would normally be thrown away.

heritage and wisdom," says Dylan Jones, who runs the restaurant with his wife, chef Bo Songvisava. At the beginning, Songvisava struggled to find certain ingredients in local markets, let alone people who knew time-honored recipes from various Thai regions, such as *Mon*-style beef curry or a *lon* of fish-sauce marinated rice. She set out to find suppliers all over the country as well as people who knew how to cook with indigenous ingredients like cassia leaves or hummingbird flowers. Today, the restaurant is a colorful celebration of Thailand's vibrant cuisine, served family-style. "It's quintessentially Thai," says Jones.

For today's forward-thinking chefs, the most important task is to keep traditions alive while also running a sustainable kitchen. If they continue to source inspiration from both the past and the future, we can all look forward to many more ambitious restaurants and cuisines. And while food scenes and restaurants always change—it is, after all, what makes them so interesting—we should take time to appreciate their heritage and the way this contributes to the sense of place that we magically feel whenever we delve deeper into a particular culture.

08 An evening meal at Bo.lan might involve ordering one of three
   set menus—the Balance, the Botanical, or the Feast—each comprised
   of a selection of little bites.

09 Desserts made with fresh ingredients are beautifully presented
   in cut glasses, like this pandan rice jelly with tropical fruit and
   coconut cream.

09

ASTAIR

by Tristan Auer

In Paris, those in the know head to Astair for a celebration of French "savoir vivre, abundance, and good taste."

Located in Paris's Passage des Panoramas, Astair takes a fresh look at the French brasserie experience. According to its owners, this is a place where Parisians can come to "eat snails in evening dress, a cocktail in hand, with jazz in the background." In order to create the right vibe, Astair enlisted the services of top interior designer Tristan Auer, renowned for his skill in combining the classic with the avant-garde. The terrazzo flooring, the banquette seating, and the bentwood cane chairs are classic, while the avant-garde cocktail bar that stands at the center of it all is whimsical and art moderne. As for the menu, all the brasserie classics are there—escargots in parsley butter, sole *meunière,* and chocolate soufflé—skillfully crafted by three-Michelin-star chef Gilles Goujon.

(below) The
creators of
Astair:
Jean-François
Monfort, Jean
Valfort,
and Charles
Drouhaut
(from left
to right).

Typical brasserie desserts include
tarte tatin, *îles flottantes*, rum baba
with fruit, and chocolate fondant.

DUDDELL'S

by Michaelis Boyd

A curious combination, Duddell's London
presents a canteen-style ambience in a historic
church setting.

A stone's throw from the Shard at London Bridge, St. Thomas's
church is a fine example of late-seventeenth-century neoclassical architecture. So it comes as a surprise to learn that it is now
home to a premium Cantonese restaurant, Duddell's of Hong
Kong. The combination may seem incongruous, but such is the
handling of the interior design by architects Michaelis Boyd,
that the two are perfectly juxtaposed. Retaining original features
that include wood paneling and impressive stained-glass windows
(albeit with clear panes), the church interior is spacious, with
stylish chandeliers suspended from the ceiling. While there is an
undeniable sense of luxury, particularly in the jade-colored
glazed tiles that line the impressively long bar, the restaurant
is far from ostentatious. Instead, banquette seating and cool geometric flooring evoke a comfortable, retro, canteen vibe.

PRADO RESTAURANTE

by Arkstudio

"If it's not in season, it's not on the table."
This is the ethos at Prado Restaurante in Lisbon,
a celebration of the best cuisine Portugal has
to offer.

This restaurant is housed in an abandoned factory that was previously derelict and overrun with vegetation. Taking their cue from the state of the place, the creative trio Isaac Almeida, Tânia Fonseca, and Marta Fonseca conceived this farm-to-table culinary venture, Prado—which translates as "meadow"—in the heart of the Portuguese capital. The trio preserved elements from the original building, including old machinery that has been restored and reassembled in its original position. The team also based its approach on nature-inspired elements, adopting a predominantly green color scheme and filling the impressive, high-ceilinged dining space with fresh produce and plants. With simple furnishings and a beautiful tiled floor, the result is an unpretentious eatery with a minimalist touch and a welcoming farm-shop vibe.

(left and opposite) From the table settings to the branding, every aspect of the Prado dining hall is minimalist, leaving diners to focus on the greenery that surrounds them.

Simple pendant light fittings are suspended from
the structural frame of the building, above blond-wood
tables and chairs.

Chef António Galapito (right) has
worked hard to forge relationships
with Portugal's best regional farmers,
fishermen, and producers.

The Prado enterprise also runs a grocery store next door to the restaurant. With the same ethos, it sells high-quality regional products.

Like the restaurant next door, the grocery store has a predominantly green and white color scheme and a beautiful tiled floor.

LA COLMADA

by Ultramarina Studio

Uniting people of all persuasions,
La Colmada heralds a new lease on life
for the Spanish *ultramarinos*.

Run by locals for locals, the quintessential Spanish grocery store has seen a decline in recent years, with owners struggling to survive the financial crisis. But things are starting to change thanks to a new generation determined to giving the concept a new lease on life. One such place is La Colmada, the brainchild of Alejandro Abades, Carlos Dorrego, and Lucía Fernández. Combining the *ultramarinos* with another long-standing Spanish tradition—the *taberna*—this is the kind of place where you drop by to stock up on manchego cheese and olives, and end up staying for lunch. Cozy, intimate, and informal, the success of this diner lies in its simple yet distinctive branding— bold typography and geometric forms. Each room is painted in a single bold color above traditional tiled floors, offsetting the shelves of beautifully packaged groceries.

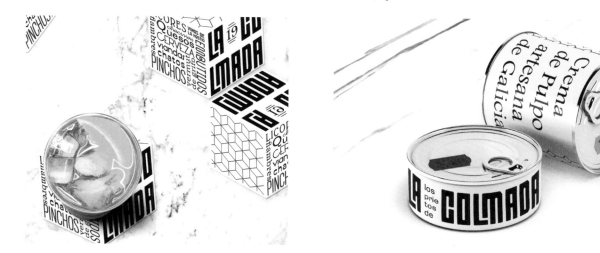

Ultramarina Studio developed a strong and striking brand identity for La Colmada, centered on a distinctive bold, black typeface, which features on the menus, products, and place settings.

SOHO'S
LITTLE
ITALY

LONDON,
U.K.

OPENING A RESTAURANT WAS THE FULFILLMENT OF A FAMILY DREAM FOR THE OWNERS OF LONDON'S RENOWNED DELICATESSEN, LINA STORES

Anyone familiar with London's Soho neighborhood will know of Lina Stores, a long-standing traditional Italian delicatessen. The store was established on Brewer Street in 1944 by Lina from Genova, whose ambition was to bring a little bit of Italy to the streets of London. Some 75 years later, Lina's descendants continue to run the store, which still stands in the same location. Along with Bar Italia, established five years later on Frith Street, it remains a Soho fixture and stands testament to the neighborhood's mid-twentieth-century Italian heritage.

Operated by a predominantly Italian team and stacked to the rafters with authentic, high-quality Italian products, from cured meat to cheese to panettone to pasta, Lina Stores is instantly recognizable by its period green-tiled and black-painted exterior. Inside this little corner shop, the walls are lined with floor-to-ceiling shelving painted pistachio green and filled with beautifully packaged goods. A marble-topped counter runs the length of the store, which is complete with refrigerated displays stocked with a tantalizing range of antipasti delights—among them the store's own homemade pasta.

Fans of this gastronomic haven will be delighted to discover that Lina Stores recently opened a restaurant in the same spirit as the delicatessen, also in Soho, just up the road on Greek Street: "We've been toying with the idea of opening a restaurant for years really—75 to be exact—but we were waiting for the perfect time to do so. We wanted to open something that respects and embraces this

The restaurant presents traditional Italian recipes including these ricotta and herb *gnudi* with sage and brown butter.

The barman fixes a Lina Stores Negroni cocktail—a heady combination of Campari, red vermouth, and gin.

"WE'VE BEEN TOYING WITH THE IDEA OF OPENING A RESTAURANT FOR YEARS, BUT WE WERE WAITING FOR THE PERFECT TIME TO DO SO."

Lina Stores offers the famous Bellini cocktail: blood orange, prosecco, and Fernet-Branca liqueur.

There is a comforting retro vibe in the little touches, such as the daily newspaper hanging ready for reading.

long-standing Italian influence in the city, and continues it in a way that innovates and takes that history on board," says head chef, Masha Rener. With a menu centered on products from the store, the focus here is on fine Italian fare, delivered with a warm smile.

Working with London-based brand-identity specialists Everything in Between and architects Red Deer, the family was intent on creating a restaurant interior that follows that of the original delicatessen: "For years people have known our deli for its pistachio-green interiors, white marble counters, and vintage style. It's something that transports us back to that time when Lina Stores first opened, and that old-time charm is something we want to keep," adds Rener. The designers adopted elements of 1950s styling to give the two-story restaurant a vintage look and to create the impression that the place has been there for decades. At street level, a 1950s-style, aluminum-edged counter undulates through the restaurant, which diners can sit at on upholstered stools.

Downstairs, below a vaulted ceiling the restaurant walls are part-tiled in the brand's signature pistachio green. Above this, black-and-white photos of the delicatessen over the years hang on roughly plastered, whitewashed walls. Diners sit on Formica-upholstered, chrome-framed chairs at marble-topped tables—the menus, the globe lights, the crockery—matching the Lina Stores aesthetic and color-scheme. The look is clean, bright, and fresh. On the street, below a green-and-white striped

An Italian classic: ribbons of pappardelle pasta, with slow-cooked veal ragu seasoned with rosemary and sage.

"WHEN GUESTS HEAR THAT THEY CAN BUY OUR HANDMADE PASTA, IT ENCOURAGES THEM TO LEARN MORE ABOUT ITALIAN CUISINE."

Lina Stores has long been renowned for its homemade pasta. Available in the delicatessen for many years, it now also features on the restaurant menu.

awning that matches the tiled floor inside, the shop signage mirrors that of the store in Brewer Street, in bold black letters and sans serif typeface. A charming finishing touch is the tiled pavement outside the restaurant, which has a mosaic design with the company's name.

While Italian food can be found throughout London, Lina Stores has the edge because the vast majority of the dishes use products and ingredients from the deli—an important aspect of the venture for the store's owners since it makes customers feel that they can recreate their favorite dishes themselves. "When guests hear that they can buy the handmade pasta in the deli to take home, it really encourages them to get creative and learn more about Italian cuisine along the way," explains Rener. Lina Stores excels when it comes to making handmade pasta—something that diners delight in watching being produced in the open-plan restaurant kitchen.

Lina Stores's novel presentation of lemon sorbet, served in a halved lemon shell with a glass of limoncello liqueur.

THE FOCUS HERE IS ON
FINE ITALIAN FARE DELIVERED
WITH A WARM SMILE.

Aqua-blue mosaic tiles beneath a 1940s art-deco mirror—even the washrooms have been styled to reflect the period interior of the original delicatessen.

AIMO E NADIA BISTRO

by Rossana Orlandi

A unique melding of creative minds sets
the scene for this unusual Italian bistro in
the heart of Milan.

In a collaborative venture that exudes Italian flair, Aimo e Nadia bistRo is a fusion of regional Italian cuisine and avant-garde gallery design. The restaurant is the brainchild of two-Michelin-star chefs, Fabio Pisani and Alessandro Negrini, founders of Il Luogo di Aimo e Nadia, and the visionary creative Rossana Orlandi, owner of the adjoining gallery. Diners are invited to choose from a varied menu tailored to the demands of urban living, against a backdrop of stunning Etro Home wallpapers and textiles. Embracing sumptuousness to the fullest, the interior is a medley of color, pattern, and texture, against which Orlandi has set an eclectic range of vintage and contemporary furnishings. It's a novel approach that brings a vibrant visual dimension to the dining experience.

Among the simple desserts served here are caramelized apple with lemon cream and buckwheat biscuit, and a carpaccio of pineapple with star anise (pictured).

OPEN

FÜR SIE GEÖFFNET

DI BIS FR 09.00 – 18.00 UHR
SA UND SO 10.00 – 17.00 UHR

MONTAG IST RUHETAG

CREMEDELACREME.AT

CRÈME DE LA CRÈME

by Bureau Rabensteiner

Located in the heart of Vienna and laced with
French flair, Crème de la Crème is a true champion
of holistic branding.

Stepping into this elegant patisserie is like finding yourself
suddenly miniaturized and nestled inside one of its stylish
takeaway boxes packed with the finest handmade pastries.
With an interior conceived by graphic design studio Bureau
Rabensteiner, Crème de la Crème exhibits holistic branding at
its best. Everything in this café is created with the same
attention to detail, craftsmanship, and finesse as the food itself.
There is precision in the arrangement of the classic Thonet
bentwood chairs around the bistro tables and in the neat
botanical display, with its grid of little brass shelves. From the
signage to the coffee cups, the paper bags to the coasters,
the branding blends minimalism with art-deco flair in a tasteful
palette of cream, gold, and dark emerald green.

21 GRAMM

On the wall above the kitchen, a faded verse from the Bible reads: "What I do, you do not know now, but you will find out afterwards. John 13.7." Perhaps a fitting mantra for this venture, the verse being one of several original features unearthed during the conversion of this former chapel into a brunch and dinner spot. Its three founders—a holy trinity, if you like—embraced the building's historic past in forging its future, deliberately keeping modern elements detached from the original structure. In this room within a room, custom-made fixtures and fittings sit comfortably amid salmon-pink columns that support lofty vaulted ceilings. Meanwhile, a judicious use of greenery echoes the rambling foliage of the adjacent cemetery. Eating a wholesome breakfast is a feel-good experience and even the bar's name has a spiritual connotation, 21 grams being the supposed weight of one's soul.

An old chapel makes for an unusual setting for 21 Gramm in Berlin's Neukölln neighborhood.

An outdoor terrace runs beneath the building's brickwork colonnade, with a wooden deck and umbrella-shaded tables.

Much of the furniture at 21 Gramm is bespoke. The planted pendant lamps were designed by the owners and a metalworker friend made the table legs.

Simple tables and chairs fill the central space at 21 Gramm. Patrons can also lounge on the less formal bench seating around the edges of the room.

RAW,
PURE
LOCAL

ZEALAND,
DENMARK

WITH AN EMPHASIS ON CONTEMPORARY NORDIC CUISINE, THE PHILOSOPHY AT DRAGSHOLM SLOT IS DRIVEN BY ITS PROXIMITY TO NATURE

Dragsholm Castle lies on the Odsherred Peninsula in northwest Zealand, an hour's drive from the Danish capital. Wild and largely untouched for centuries, this region marks the country's first (and only) UNESCO-appointed Geopark. Immediately surrounding the castle are rolling hills that were formed during the glacial activity of the last Ice Age. To the east, open meadows gradually give way to the flatlands of the Lammefjord and, beyond that, the fjord itself. This land, once below sea level, was reclaimed during the nineteenth century and has extremely fertile soil as a result. It is against this backdrop that the castle functions, today, as a boutique hotel and center of Nordic cuisine. The region is particularly renowned for its cultivation of herbs and vegetables, and the rolling hills, forests, and bays are teeming with flora and fauna. For the owners of Dragsholm Slot, these ancient, natural surroundings are key to their ethos: "Our ambition was, is, and will remain to create, maintain, and develop a local cuisine that cultivates the story and the specific characteristics and qualities of our own terrain," says project manager, Thomas Kjelfred.

The earliest records of a castle on this site date back to 1215, while the current building—solid, white, and baroque in style—dates from around the turn of the eighteenth century. Also historic, is the herb garden, which plays a central role in the gastronomy of the restaurants here. First established by the monks who inhabited the castle in the Middle Ages, the garden was revived at the turn of the

In keeping with the castle's ethos, the interior decoration is also raw, pure, and simple. Below, the simply designed wooden furniture and neutral, rough-plastered walls of the bistro.

View looking through the castle's entranceway and out across the untamed Lammefjord landscape.

ROOTS, SHOOTS,
FLOWERS, LEAVES,
AND SEEDS
REGULARLY FIND
THEIR WAY
INTO THE DISHES
CRAFTED IN THE
HOTEL KITCHENS.

Bottles of herb-infused oils,
essences, and dressings.

A healthy looking bunch of
wild cicely, freshly picked in
the castle's herb garden.

twenty-first century. While its original purpose was to provide all manner of herbs for medicinal uses, the garden now supplies the hotel with more than 100 plant species. In tune with the cycle of seasons, the plants are used in all phases of their growth: "No time of year nor season are the same in Lammefjorden; nothing can be planned in advance in the kitchen. We adapt to the whims of nature and the season's harvest, and we work with the many varieties of fruits and vegetables and their different flavors in the many stages of development," explains head chef Claus Henriksen. Roots, shoots, flowers, leaves, and seeds regularly find their way into the dishes crafted in the hotel kitchens. In addition to this bounty, the hotel is deeply committed to foraging the wilds of the region for additional seasonal ingredients: "The herbs, mushrooms, and vegetables that we pick in the fields, in the forest and on the beach contribute constantly to new dishes and new taste experiences," adds Henriksen.

The guiding light at the hotel's restaurants is Claus Henriksen, who has worked at Copenhagen's Formula B and Noma restaurants. The shift from urban to rural had a profound effect on the chef: "I fell in love with the DNA of the place. In the ambition, in the surrounding fields and forests, and the entire area. Near to the local produce and the soil, ... I can see them evolve day by day, watch them germinate and grow and experience the evolution of their taste." The philosophy of the cuisine at Dragsholm Slot was second nature to Henriksen, as he had previously created Nordic dishes with fresh

There is an air of tranquility at Dragsholm Slot, instilled by the calm of the open landscape beyond.

FOR THE OWNERS OF DRAGSHOLM SLOT, ITS ANCIENT, NATURAL SURROUNDINGS ARE KEY TO THEIR ETHOS.

and foraged ingredients in the city, and it quickly took root in the hotel's two restaurants. Spisehuset, an informal bistro, offers modern interpretations of classic Nordic recipes dishes, while Slotskøkkenet takes a more gourmet approach and is altogether more innovative and experimental. At the heart of both is this essential focus on natural, seasonal, local foods sourced from the garden and foraged from the Lammefjord and Odsherred's forests, fields, and beaches. In the words of the chef himself, "We have a logical mindset telling us to cook using local produce in season … For us Lammefjord is our treasure trove which stores amazing stories and endless potential to create dishes with reference to a very long history. We have just started to discover them."

A selection of handpicked herbs and vegetables from the garden in cludes baby carrots, potatoes, scallions, nasturtiums, and wild strawberries.

A red-tinged potted-plant display stands on the windowsill in the Spisehuset bistro, the only accent of color in the light-filled room.

"WE HAVE A LOGICAL MINDSET TELLING US TO COOK USING LOCAL PRODUCE IN THE SEASON."
—CLAUS HENRIKSEN

MOSQUITO SUPPER CLUB

Three nights a week, Mosquito Supper Club treats locals
to a five-course celebration of Cajun cuisine.

Having witnessed the demise of many childhood traditions, Melissa Martin
established the Mosquito Supper Club in a bid to keep homemade Cajun
food on the menu. Occupying the ground floor of a quaint wood-frame house
in New Orleans's Milan neighborhood, Martin's restaurant is simply
decorated with scrubbed wooden floors and earth-toned fixtures and fittings.
She conjures a parlor-style atmosphere in which diners sit elbow to elbow
on benches at farmhouse tables. Each sitting, hosted on Thursday, Friday,
and Saturday evenings, serves just 24 diners a five-course menu based
on the bounty of local shrimpers, crabbers, oystermen, and farmers. Foodies
tuck in to crawfish *boulettes,* shrimp and okra gumbo, soft-shell crabs,
and home-baked fruit pies in an intimate dining experience that will be
remembered.

Melissa Martin's sensitivity in creating a parlor-style ambience
leaves guests feeling that they have dined in a private home.

CHINA CHILCANO

by Capella Garcia Arquitectura

Three is the magic number at China Chilcano, a contemporary Peruvian restaurant in the heart of Penn Quarter, Washington D.C.

This eclectic restaurant is a celebration of Peru's deeply rooted and diverse culinary heritage. Centering on native Criollo, Chinese Chifa, and Japanese Nikkei influences, dishes explore the crossover between these three distinct cultures. Diners delight at traditional Peruvian stews on the menu alongside *nigiri* and *dim sum*. Dominated by a vibrant floral mural on the far wall and furnished with numerous scatter cushions in colorful Peruvian textiles, the restaurant also has three distinct dining areas. The main area has clusters of tables with beautiful, low hanging, red glass pendant lights. A bar to the side has a wood-and-rope structure reminiscent of shipping containers, while a third section is home to a sushi counter and a Japanese *tatami* table. Overhead, neon lights are shaped like the ancient geoglyphs etched into the Peruvian landscape.

PATENT PENDING

by Carpenter + Mason

Concealed behind a chic café just north of
Madison Square Park lies a low-lit cocktail bar with
an electrifying theme.

The Radio Wave Building in New York's up-and-coming NoMad district used
to be the Gerlach Hotel. It was renamed in honor of the radio wave pioneer
Nikola Tesla, who lived and worked here in the 1890s. Down in the basement, come 5 p.m., a "secret" accordion door opens to reveal a seductive
Tesla-themed bar—a speakeasy where it is always cocktail time. Fashioned
by Ryan McKenzie at Simmer Group, intimate booths upholstered in
emerald-green vinyl are juxtaposed with blackened bare-brick walls and an
array of chrome-top bulbs hang from the ceiling above the bar. A dim,
seductive glow creates a relaxed ambience as guests choose cocktails from
menus designed to look like pages from one of Tesla's notebooks. Those
who know about Tesla will spot that the drinks are named after key events
in the "Electric Messiah's" life.

Both the interior design and branding are slick. Predominantly dark surfaces glimmer in the low light, and even the ice cubes are embossed with the bars "PP" logo.

ANNOYED BY RESTAURANT PLAYLISTS,

A MASTER MUSICIAN MADE HIS OWN

HOW RYUICHI SAKAMOTO ASSEMBLED THE SOUNDTRACK FOR KAJITSU, IN MURRAY HILL, AND WHAT IT SAYS ABOUT THE SOUNDS WE HEAR (OR SHOULD) WHILE WE EAT

NEW YORK,
USA

187

Last fall a friend told me a story about Ryuichi Sakamoto, the renowned musician and composer who lives in the West Village. Mr. Sakamoto, it seems, so likes a particular Japanese restaurant in Murray Hill, and visits it so often, that he finally had to be straight with the chef: He could not bear the music it played for its patrons.

The issue was not so much that the music was loud, but that it was thoughtless. Mr. Sakamoto suggested that he could take over the job of choosing it, without pay, if only so he could feel more comfortable eating there. The chef agreed, and so Mr. Sakamoto started making playlists for the restaurant, none of which include any of his own music. Few people knew about this, because Mr. Sakamoto has no particular desire to publicize it.

It took me a few weeks to appreciate how radical the story was, if indeed it was true. I consider thoughtless music in restaurants a problem that has gotten worse over the years, even since the advent of the music-streaming services, which—you'd think—should have made it better.

If I'm going to spend decent money on a meal, I don't want the reservation-taker, the dishwasher or someone from the back office to be cooking it; I want someone who is very good at cooking food to do it. The same should apply to the music, which after all will be playing before, during and after the eating.

I would prefer that music not seem an afterthought, or the result of algorithmic computation. I want it chosen by a person who knows music up and down and sideways: its context, its dynamism and its historical and aural clichés. Such a person can at least accomplish the minimum, which is to signal to the customer that attention is being paid, in a generous, original, specific and small-ego way.

In February, I went to Mr. Sakamoto's favorite restaurant, on 39th Street near Lexington Avenue, with my younger son. It is a split-level operation: On the second floor is Kajitsu, which follows the Zen, vegan principles of Shojin cuisine, and on the ground floor is Kokage, a more casual operation that incorporates meat and fish into the same idea. (A Japanese tea shop, Ippodo, occupies a counter toward the front of the street-level space.)

As soon as we sat down, the music pinned our attention. It came from an unpretentious source—a single, wide speaker sitting on a riser about a foot off the floor, hidden behind a serving table. (We were downstairs in Kokage, but the same music was playing upstairs in Kajitsu.) I asked a waiter if the playlist was Mr. Sakamoto's. She said yes.

Mr. Sakamoto, 66, is exemplary perhaps not only for his music but also for his listening, and his understanding of how music can be used and shared. He is a hero of cosmopolitan musical curiosity, an early technological adopter in extremis, and a kind of supercollaborator. Since the late 1970s, when he was a founding member of the electronic-pop trio Yellow Magic Orchestra, he has composed and produced music for dance floors, concert halls, films, video

Mr. Sakamoto's soundtrack plays in Kokage and upstairs at Kajitsu, above. "The color of the wall, the texture of the furniture, the setting of the room, wasn't good for enjoying music with darker tones," said Norika Sora, Mr. Sakamoto's manager and wife.

games, cellphone ringtones, and acts of ecological awareness and political resistance. (Much of this is detailed in "Coda," Stephen Nomura Schible's recently released film documentary about him.)

Some of what we heard at Kokage sounded like what Mr. Sakamoto would logically be interested in. There was slow or spacious solo-piano music from various indistinct traditions; a few melodies that might have been film-soundtrack themes; a bit of improvisation. Where there was singing, it was generally not in English. I recognized a track from Wayne Shorter's record "Native Dancer," with Milton Nascimento, and a pianist who sounded like Mary Lou Williams, although I couldn't be sure. This wasn't particularly brand-establishing music, or the kind that makes you want to spend money; it represented a devoted customer's deep knowledge, sensitivity and idiosyncrasies. I felt generally stumped and sensitively attended to. I felt ecstatic.

I found out that Mr. Sakamoto had enlisted Ryu Takahashi, a New York music producer, manager and curator, to help him with the playlist. My son and I met them both, as well as Norika Sora, Mr. Sakamoto's wife and manager, on a bright spring afternoon between services at Kajitsu, where the tobacco-earth smell of Iribancha tea permeated the dining room. Mr. Sakamoto was dressed in black down to his sneakers.

I asked if the story I'd heard was true. It was, he said. I asked if it would bother him if people knew.

"It's O.K.," he said. "We don't have to hide."

He is not in the habit of complaining when he has a problem with music in public spaces, because it happens so often. "Normally I just leave," he said. "I cannot bear it. But this restaurant is really something I like, and I respect their chef, Odo." (Hiroki Odo was Kajitsu's third chef, and worked there for five years, until March. Mr. Odo told me the music had been chosen by the restaurant's management in Japan.)

"I found their BGM so bad, so bad," Mr. Sakamoto said, using the industry term for background music. ("BGM" was also the title of a Yellow Magic Orchestra record from 1981.) He sucked his teeth. "Really bad." What was it? "It was a mixture of terrible Brazilian pop music and some old American folk music," he said, "and some jazz, like Miles Davis."

Some of those things, individually, may be very good, I suggested.

"If they have context, maybe," he replied. "But at least the Brazilian pop was so bad. I know Brazilian music. I have worked with Brazilians many times. This was so bad. I couldn't stay, one afternoon. So I left."

He went home and composed an email to Mr. Odo. "I love your food, I respect you and I love this restaurant, but I hate the music," he remembered writing. "Who chose this? Whose decision of mixing this terrible round-up? Let me do it. Because your food is as good as the beauty of Katsura Rikyu." (He meant the thousand-year-old palatial villa in Kyoto, built to some degree on the aesthetic

Fine details at Kajitsu: a cup of tea.

principles of imperfections and natural circumstances known as wabi-sabi.) "But the music in your restaurant is like Trump Tower."

A bad musical experience in a restaurant these days may be a kind of imitation of a thoughtful one, or at least a sufficient one: a good-enough one. It can be the result of the algorithmic programming from, say, a Pandora or Spotify station. It can be one of the many playlists made by human curators at one of those streaming services, meant for broad appeal. Or it can be the result of the safe or self-absorbed choices from someone in the restaurant. As with restaurant food, so with restaurant music: Good-enough isn't good enough.

I asked a few restaurateurs how they get beyond the good-enough in creating or controlling their own playlists. Gerardo Gonzalez, the chef at Lalito, in Chinatown, spoke of first encounters and parting impressions. He contends that music is the first and strongest sensory indicator of what a restaurant is about; he wants his customers to leave in a better mood than that in which they entered.

Well-known tracks, he suggested, can be useful. But some feeling of lift or transcendence is essential. (He cited the jazz-harp music of Alice Coltrane and Dorothy Ashby as examples of music that does not go wrong.) Also, a great playlist for your customers is not equal to the music you listen to for own purposes. "I draw the line," he specified, "at something I might listen to at home, which might be bleak and dystopic."

Brooks Headley, the chef of Superiority Burger in the East Village, and a musician himself—he has played drums in punk bands since the early '90s—sent an iPod around to some discerning friends so they could load it up with their suggestions. "Nothing too moody or serious," he cautioned them. They took his request seriously, and he likes not knowing everything that plays. (A hit in his restaurant: the album "Rock and Rollin' With Fats Domino," played in its entirety, all 29 minutes.)

Frank Falcinelli, a chef and partner at Prime Meats and the Frankies restaurants in New York, dreads restaurant-music clichés, and has developed ways to avoid them: playing original versions of songs made much more famous by covers, or playing deep cuts from well-known popular records. For instance: "Moonlight Mile," from the Rolling Stones album "Sticky Fingers," but not "Brown Sugar." (Please, not "Brown Sugar.")

Siobhan Lowe, manager of the restaurant (Reynard) and bar (The Ides) in the Wythe Hotel in Brooklyn, hired the sound-design firm Gray V to make its varied and frequently updated playlists. She will give instructions— "make a playlist for a rainy afternoon in the Ides that would not freak out my dad but that music nerds will be impressed by"—and then lets the experts do their work. Like Mr. Falcinelli, she has seen the seductive power of the deep cut over her customers: Her example was a live version of Talking Heads's "The Big Country."

I asked Mr. Sakamoto whether the exercise of creating a restaurant

playlist was as simple as choosing music he liked. "No," he said. "In the beginning, I wanted to have a collection of ambient music—not Brian Eno, but more recent." He came to the restaurant and listened carefully as he ate. He and his wife agreed that the music was much too dark in mood.

"The light is pretty bright here," Ms. Sora said. "The color of the wall, the texture of the furniture, the setting of the room, wasn't good for enjoying music with darker tones, to end your night. I think it depends not just on the food or the hour of the day, but the atmosphere, the color, the decoration."

Mr. Takahashi reckoned that he and Mr. Sakamoto made at least five drafts before settling on the current version of the Kajitsu playlist. Some songs were too this or too that—too loud, too bright, too "jazzy."

"Playing jazz in restaurants is too stereotypical," Mr. Sakamoto said. Jazz pianists are a particularly vexed issue for him. You will hear Mary Lou Williams, but not (at this point, anyway) Duke Ellington. You will hear Bill Evans, but not his famous "Waltz for Debby." You will hear solo Jason Moran and Thelonious Monk.

One of the solo-piano songs that slayed me turned out to be the first movement of John Cage's serene "Four Walls," played by Aki Takahashi. ("It's so pop," Mr. Sakamoto marveled. "It's like a radio hit.") Another was Gavin Bryars's "My First Homage." A few others that moved me, piano or not: David Shire's "Graysmith's Theme," from the score to the film "Zodiac"; Roberto Musci's "Claudia, Wilhelm R and Me." All of

this music stood at a particular angle with regard to the listener: It was riveting, moderate and unobtrusive.

It was also not very loud, and here we arrive at an issue that may concern older customers more than younger ones. Mr. Sakamoto objects to loud restaurant music, and often uses a decibel meter on his phone to measure the volume of the sound around him.

He has composed original music for public spaces before, he said—a scientific museum and an advertising-agency building in Tokyo. He used light and wind sensors to change the music during the day. But the only experience he has had making playlists of the music of others, for other people, has been for family members.

He made one for his son, when he was learning to play the bass guitar; Mr. Sakamoto carefully excluded the bassist Jaco Pastorius, for reasons of personal taste, but his son found out about Mr. Pastorius a week later and scolded his father for the omission. Mr. Sakamoto made one for his father, during a hospital illness. And he made one for his mother's funeral.

Was that, I asked, a collection of music she liked? Mr. Sakamoto paused and laughed and shook his head. "It was, kind of, my ego," he said.

Mr. Sakamoto and Mr. Takahashi plan to change their playlist with each new season. Mr. Odo's next venture, a bar named Hall and a restaurant named Odo, is scheduled to open in the Flatiron district in the fall. Mr. Sakamoto, again, has been retained as chief playlister.

Kokage by Kajitsu
The non-vegetarian restaurant

~ Lunch 11:45 am - 1:45 pm ~
Closed Monday, Sunday & every 1st day of the month
~ Dinner 5:3 10:00 pm ~
Closed Mo

212-228-4873
125 East 39th Street
New York, NY 10016
(Between Park & Lexington Avenue)

GO GREEN IN

THE KITCHEN

Sustainability is at the heart of a new global food culture. From sourcing ingredients and respecting the well-being of food producers, to seeing the culinary potential of "waste" ingredients, chefs are reexamining every aspect of the food supply chain. Together they are trying to make the culinary world better for both people and the planet.

A new generation of chefs are taking a stand on sustainability—sourcing, using, and, in some cases, re-using ingredients in increasingly imaginative ways. Sustainability is fast becoming the basis of a code of conduct followed by some of the world's best restaurants—at heart, sustainability demands consideration of every aspect of the food supply chain. Many of these chefs are based in Scandinavia, either alumni of René Redzepi's celebrated Copenhagen restaurant Noma or influenced and inspired by the groundbreaking New Nordic cuisine that it pioneered. All of them are breaking the mold to redefine what high-end restaurants can do to help create a more sustainable food industry.

"We have set out on a journey that we hope will make an impact on both the restaurant industry and how people approach cooking every day," explains Matt Orlando, the founder of Amass, an acclaimed restaurant in Copenhagen, where finding creative ways to combat food waste is practically a philosophy. Caring about how your ingredients are sourced is one aspect of running a sustainable kitchen, but so is caring about what happens to them once you've used them.

Orlando, a former head chef at Noma, opened Amass in a run-down waterfront district of the Danish capital in 2014. Blessed with plenty of outdoor space, he and his team built a greenhouse and a large kitchen garden that supplies the restaurant with leafy greens, vegetables, and edible flowers. However, Orlando also became increasingly aware of the amount of waste and leftovers generated at Amass. Having set out to give diners a great culinary experience, he and his team realized they had a bigger mission.

In short, Orlando has adopted a more holistic approach to cuisine and is on a constant mission to minimize his restaurant's food waste and make better use of leftovers. That means, for instance, turning skins, seeds, and stems into dried seasonings or chips; or replacing tea with infusions made from dried herbs, fruits, and flowers from the garden; or reusing coffee grounds to make cookies. Meanwhile, Orlando's success with composting means Amass hasn't had to throw away any organic waste since it opened.

Further north in Scandinavia, another determined chef is working on "closing the loop."
Paul Svensson runs Fotografiska, a restaurant located in a photography museum in Stockholm.
It's a place not only for people with an interest in contemporary photography, but also for conscientious foodies. Dishes are

At Amass, finding creative ways to combat food waste is practically a philosophy. Caring about how your ingredients are sourced is one aspect of running a sustainable kitchen, but so is caring about what happens to them once you've used them.

plant-based with an emphasis on local, seasonal ingredients. And, like Orlando, Svensson has a zero-waste philosophy: his kitchen uses each and every part of an ingredient to try to provide the best possible flavor. By questioning why we discard some things but consider others delicacies, Svensson has helped put food waste on the agenda in Sweden. From vegetable peels to fish scales to mozzarella brine, Svensson uses ingredients that others would consider waste, whether in preserves, extracts, drinks, or purées.

01   QO Hotel runs a circular greenhouse system, making it wholly
      sustainable. Everything produced here gets used in the hotel.

Closing the Loop

In the spring of 2018, a restaurant in Amsterdam took sustainability to a whole new level—quite literally. Located on the ground floor of the QO Hotel, Persijn sources many of its ingredients from the greenhouse on the rooftop. As well as more than 70 varieties of fruit, vegetables, herbs and flowers, the greenhouse allows diners to enjoy what it calls "fish to fork" cuisine. That's because it boasts an aquaponic system: tanks containing fish whose waste provides an organic source of food for the plants, which in turn purify the water for the fish. And once the fish—a fatty species of tiger bass known as omega perch—reach the end of their natural life cycle, they can be used in the kitchen.

02

"We have set out on a journey that we hope will make an impact on both the restaurant industry and how people approach cooking every day."—Matt Orlando, founder of Amass.

02 Matt Orlando, chef and owner of Amass, has been fine-tuning his approach to sustainability since the restaurant's inception in 2013.

03 The Amass restaurant garden grows eighty different plant varieties. They include leafy vegetables, berries, herbs, and flowers, some of which appear on their daily menu.

Thinking Local

Browse the menu in most decent restaurants today, and you'll likely spot the word "local." Whether it's organic vegetables grown in the kitchen garden, cuts of meat from animals raised in nearby pastures, or single-origin coffee delivered by the artisanal roaster around the corner, the importance of provenance and sustainability—and sourcing local ingredients in particular—has gone mainstream.

Indeed, a decade ago, only the most forward-thinking establishments adhered to this philosophy. But in recent years, amid growing concern about climate change and the impact of the food industry, the locavore food movement has spread throughout the gastronomic world. Far from having just a couple of local ingredients on their menus, increasing numbers of chefs and restaurateurs are openly acknowledging their responsibility

05

to the planet and taking their impact on the environment more seriously.

Take Christian Puglisi, a former Noma sous-chef and the owner of several bars, bakeries, and restaurants in Copenhagen. In 2016 he launched Farm of Ideas, a 70-acre (30-hectare) organic farm just outside the Danish capital. Dubbed "a melting pot for innovation, gastronomy, community, and sustainable agriculture," Farm of Ideas supplies vegetables, raw milk, eggs, and meat to Puglisi's restaurants, including Relæ—twice the winner of a prestigious award for the world's most sustainable restaurant.

Puglisi has said his aim is to "farm smart and farm differently"—in other words, "to grow better not bigger." His plan has already succeeded in one important respect: chefs at his four Copenhagen restaurants believe the healthiness of the farm's soil has had a direct effect on the taste of its vegetables, making their flavor more intense.

04

04   London's Farmacy offers plant-based dishes that are free from dairy, refined sugars, additives, and chemicals.

05   Amass uses its garden as an educational tool to introduce visitors to their sustainable agriculture initiatives.

Getting the Public Involved

Of course, restaurants alone won't create a more sustainable food system. Engaging the public and building community is vital, too. Here, as well, chefs are leading the charge. In 2017 and 2018, Puglisi invited the public to visit Farm of Ideas and attend Seed Exchange, a free festival that brings together local farmers, producers, and top chefs, and aims to spark inspiration about sustainability in the food industry. It also gives children and adults a chance to go on guided tours of the farm and get a closer look at its crops and animals, thus encouraging a deeper understanding of the food served in restaurants. Sustainability is also about creating value for local communities by educating people about food and inviting them to play a bigger role in the culinary world.

06 Svensson has helped put food waste on the agenda in Sweden. From vegetable peels, to fish scales, to mozzarella brine, Svensson uses ingredients that others would consider waste, whether in preserves, extracts, drinks, or purées.

06 Paul Svensson at work in the kitchen of plant-based restaurant Fotografiska in Stockholm.

07 The food served up at Fotografiska is strictly seasonal and almost exclusively plant based. Seasonal regulars include beet, sunchoke, celeriac, and cabbage.

A Holistic Approach

There's no silver bullet that can solve the biggest problems in the food industry, including how to make it more sustainable. But initiatives such as Seed Exchange demonstrate the links in the food chain instead of only seeing the finished product on a plate. Education is imperative in helping people generate a more thoughtful relationship with ingredients and those who produce them. Farm by farm, garden by garden, dish by dish, ingredient by ingredient, the culinary world is not only changing what we eat, but leading by example to pave the way to a more sustainable world.

08

Education is imperative in helping people generate a more thoughtful relationship with ingredients and those who produce them.

09

08   Italian-born Christian Puglisi worked for a while at Noma before opening his own restaurant, Relæ, in 2010.

09   Little goes to waste in the kitchens at Dragsholm Slot. Surplus foods grown in the herb garden are frequently pickled in jars.

10 At Relæ, it is not uncommon for the humblest ingredient to take center stage, as seen here with their steamed onion with birch water and pine dish.

VÄKST

by Genbyg

In the charming Latin Quarter of Copenhagen, restaurant Väkst focuses on local greens and a cozy, relaxed vibe.

Like being invited to a garden party, restaurant Väkst sets the mood with light bulbs hanging from the ceiling and an interior greenhouse filled with plants. "Väkst" means "growth" or "plant" in Danish, and local restaurant group Cofoco embodies this in one of their newest additions to the Copenhagen restaurant scene. The menu focuses on local vegetables and seasonal herbs—with quality steak, seafood, and roasted fish available too. Located in the picturesque Latin Quarter of central Copenhagen, Väkst is part of the hip boutique hotel SP34, and both Copenhageners and visitors from all over the world dine here. Besides offering a predominantly vegetarian menu, sustainability is also represented in the materials used to design this space. Concrete walls and lamps made from antique milk cans contrast with the warm 1960s-style wooden chairs sourced from a high school in Denmark.

The restaurant is arranged over two levels—the ground floor (pictured) and a basement space.

To access the basement level, you pass through a greenhouse in the middle of the restaurant, filled with hanging baskets.

SALAD JUNGLE

Giving new meaning to "urban jungle," this bright and breezy salad bar brings zesty West Coast salad bowls to the streets of Vienna.

Before Salad Jungle opened its doors in 2017, an affordable lunch and a wholesome salad were hard to come by in the Austrian capital. Thankfully, this vibrant venue has filled the gap, offering a fresh alternative to the city's takeout options. With a youthful edge, the salad bar features a fantastic jungle mural above pristine white tiles, which is echoed in the numerous potted plants that adorn the place. Above the bar, the salad options and bowls are written in chalk on blackboards, offering a good range of tantalizing vegetarian and vegan options. The plates of fresh and tangy ingredients are generous and beautifully prepared. There's only room enough for eight eat-in diners, but with Vienna's Stadtpark just a stone's throw away, Salad Jungle caters to picnickers too.

BABEL

With its "pick, clean, and serve" ethos, this
restaurant in the South African Cape countryside
epitomizes the farm-to-fork philosophy.

A portrait of a cow adorns a white-tiled wall—a visual reminder that Babel Restaurant was once a cowshed. Floor-to-ceiling windows flood the room with natural light. On polished concrete floors, diners sit at farmyard tables spread with crisp white linen. This eatery is one of several enterprises at Babylonstoren, a historic Cape Dutch farmstead in the wine country of the Cape. The stunning gardens were designed by Patrice Taravella, owner of Prieuré Notre Dame d'Orsan in France. Inspired by the neoclassical French model, regimented gravel paths, pergolas, and water canals divide the garden into distinct sections where fruit, berries, indigenous plants, and trees grow. All activity at Babylonstoren revolves around this garden, not least the menu at Babel. Strictly seasonal, beautifully presented dishes are centered on ingredients harvested in the garden.

Diners at Babel tuck into a feast of dishes served with a range of seasonal vegetable sides in keeping with the restaurant's farm-to-table philosophy.

A winter dish of citrus-roasted pork belly with quince and *membrillo* served on vibrant green leaves of savoy cabbage.

A young boy helps to collect eggs from the chicken coop. Besides chickens, the farm also keeps bees, cattle, and ducks.

The kitchen at Babylonstoren bakes all its own bread and makes its own handcrafted cheeses—ricotta, mozzarella, and feta among them (above).

The restaurant has its own meat room in which it prepares fresh sausages, *biltong*, *droëwors*, and pickled and smoked bacon.

KIIN KIIN BAO BAO

Pan-Asian-style dishes ideal for sharing and
cocktails served within a thoughtfully
designed interior set the scene for Copenhagen's
new *bao* restaurant.

Located on the buzzing main street of Copenhagen's trendy
neighborhood Vesterbro, Kiin Kiin Bao Bao is Danish chef,
Henrik Yde's latest venture. Having earned a Michelin star
with his first restaurant Kiin Kiin, one of the few Michelin-star
Thai restaurants in the world, Yde has now expanded his
repertoire with Asian tapas-style food at Kiin Kiin Bao Bao.
Local design company Broste collaborated with Yde on
the space, interpreting modern Scandinavian design with
Asian details. Inspired by the Danish architect Arne Jacobsen,
wood-paneled walls, chairs, and benches upholstered in
russet red leather are combined with oriental details like an
abundance of cacti, brass tableware, and a random grouping
of delicate bamboo lamps suspended from the ceiling, which
create a warm and cozy atmosphere.

HIGH-ALTITUDE DINING

CUSCO,
PERU

EMBODYING THE
DIVERSITY OF THE
PERUVIAN LANDSCAPE,
VIRGILIO MARTÍNEZ
HAS CREATED A
RESTAURANT INSPIRED
BY HIGH-ALTITUDE
ECOSYSTEMS. ITS
LOCATION? IN THE
HEART OF THE
HISTORICAL INCA
TERRACES IN THE
ANDES, 11,500 FEET
(3,500 METERS)
ABOVE SEA LEVEL

219

After years of researching and planning, the world-renowned chef Virgilio Martínez opened the doors to Mil in February 2018. After having earned fourth place on the World's 50 Best Restaurants list in 2012 for his Lima-based restaurant Central, Martínez soon embarked on a year-long journey around his home country. During a trip to the Moray area in the Andes, he sought new inspiration, and, venturing from the capital to the mountains, Martínez discovered a completely new way of life. He became intrigued by the farming communities around the historical terraces of the Andes; the Incas are thought to have designed these terraces in order to adapt various coastal species to high altitudes and to adapt high-altitude species to the coast. Inspired by this sophisticated agricultural practice, Martínez and his research team created a new restaurant that drew on the philosophy behind the ancestral terraces. Their aim is to encapsulate the entire ecosystem of Peru, one of the most biodiverse places on earth, on the menu.

At Mil, Martínez and his team, whose core members include his wife, Pia León in the kitchen and his sister, Malena Martínez in the research team, take localism to the absolute extreme. Nothing is flown in, shipped in, or imported here; every single ingredient is local, from the crops to the water to the salt. Mil collaborates with two indigenous communities of the Moray area. The Mullakas-Misminay and Kacllaraccay farmers have become vital in sustaining Mil as they work with the restaurant in growing native

(below) Virgilio Martínez pictured at the Andean restaurant with his sister Malena (left) and wife Pia (right).

THE AIM IS
TO ENCAPSULATE
THE ENTIRE
ECOSYSTEM OF PERU
ON THE MENU,
ONE OF EARTH'S
MOST BIODIVERSE
PLACES.

(left) Inside, the restaurant is modest and earthy. Guests are surrounded by visual reminders of the local produce.

The menu at Mil consists of eight courses, each designed to reflect an "ecosystem of elevation." Several courses are named after the ecosystem that inspired them, such as the Plateau, the Andean Forest, and the Central Andes.

potatoes in a range of varieties, roots, as well as vegetables, and Andean grains in the nearby fields. Taking part in the daily life of these communities has created a space for exchanging knowledge, which has been valuable for both sides. The harvest is divided equally between the farmer communities and Martínez's team. The former teach the Mil team about their traditional ways of farming and cultivating, whilst Martínez's research team, called *Mater*, organizes workshops in textiles and ceramics and offers the farmer communities lessons in these crafts.

In addition to the on-site fields supplying the restaurant, Mil also makes its own chocolate from scratch using cacao seeds from Cusco, and it offers guests locally harvested coffee. The alcoholic drinks served in the restaurant are high-altitude spirits produced by the in-house distillery, and throughout Mil's eight-course menu, the surrounding landscape is ever present. Each of the courses is rooted in a different ecosystem according to the altitude. They change with the climate and the land, and all ingredients are authentic and local. It's not always about the taste for Martínez. Some dishes may be perceived as avant-garde or even have an uncomfortable feel to them, yet you have to taste them to truly understand Peru and the country's unique landscape. Just as the Andean people see the world in a vertical way, and not horizontally, Mil indicates the altitude in meters of the given ingredients alongside every dish on the menu as a way to remind their guests of the

A member of Martínez's team talks about the chocolate production from bean to finished product—each stage carried out at Mil.

NOTHING IS FLOWN IN, SHIPPED IN, OR IMPORTED HERE; EVERY SINGLE INGREDIENT IS LOCAL, FROM THE CROPS TO THE WATER TO THE SALT.

traditional Andean way of life. In his cooking, Martínez is known for using ingredients he has found on his adventures around Peru—ingredients that the indigenous communities have never considered using in cooking. However, Martínez is on a mission to reinvent the Peruvian cuisine and to show the world the magnificent diversity of the country's ecosystems, from the abundant fishing grounds of the Pacific to the Amazon rainforest to the Andes Mountains. He paints a picture of the country's landscape and its highly varied ecosystems, and then he translate these to his dishes, letting visitors from all over the world experience the essence of one of the most biodiverse places on earth in eight delicious courses.

MARTÍNEZ IS ON
A MISSION TO
REINVENT PERUVIAN
CUISINE AND TO
SHOW THE WORLD THE
MAGNIFICENT
DIVERSITY OF
THE COUNTRY'S
ECOSYSTEMS.

The Mil team gathers around a traditional outdoor stone oven known locally as a *huatia*, bowls of steaming food in their hands.

These ancient terraces, high up in the Andes Mountains,
are believed to have been created by the Incas.

GRAANMARKT 13

by Vincent Van Duysen

With a basement restaurant run by veggie master Seppe Nobels, "green" is the buzzword at Graanmarkt 13—and in more ways than one.

Founded by Ilse and Tim Cornelissens, the pretty Belgian townhouse at 13 Graanmarkt joins several ventures under one roof: a concept store selling sustainable wares; an exclusive apartment for rent; and an environmentally conscious restaurant. The dining takes place in the basement, in a sparse, functional restaurant run by celebrated chef Seppe Nobels. Named the "Vegetable Chef of the Year" by Gault & Millau in 2015, Nobels' ethos centers on his desire to minimize the environmental impact of his dishes. Noble has an incredible knack for producing light, veggie-centric dishes that are nevertheless rustic, nourishing, and original. The restaurant places a huge emphasis on local and seasonal ingredients: if the produce doesn't come from the restaurant's own rooftop garden, it is likely to have been sourced from a nearby farm.

In summer, guests can dine in a little courtyard tucked behind the restaurant.

Right at the top of Graanmarkt 13 is a rooftop garden, where the kitchen grows all of the herbs used in the restaurant's seasonal dishes.

Chef Seppe Nobels has forged partnerships with local market gardeners
and sources many of the ingredients for his dishes himself.

BAZAAR MAR

by Philippe Starck

Thanks to its striking nautical interior,
there are no prizes for guessing that seafood
tops the bill at Bazaar Mar in Miami.

Run by James Beard and award-winning chef José Andrés,
Bazaar Mar is situated in Miami's SLS Brickell Tower.
As in Andrés's other ventures, the focus here is on Spanish,
tapas-style dining, but with an emphasis on fish dishes,
like ceviche and sashimi. The impressive interior, conceived
by the acclaimed French designer Philippe Starck, is quite
surreal. With a slew of industrial pendant lamps above and
a richly veined marble floor below them, diners sit at marble-topped tables on upholstered sofas or white wooden chairs.
Then there's the main attraction—6,000 *azulejo* tiles lining
the walls and even the ceiling. Hand-painted in Spain, and
reminiscent of sixteenth-century blue-and-white Delft pottery,
the tiles feature designs drawn by artist Sergio Mora—a series
of fantastical maritime murals filled with mythical creatures.

FARMACY
by CADA

With its emphasis on "clean" indulgence, London's Farmacy
creates dishes that are good for the body and good for
the earth.

Green and serene is the atmosphere at this Notting Hill dining room.
Catering for a vegan and vegetarian client base, the menu offers an imaginative
collection of beautifully presented plant-based, chemical-free dishes
that range from probiotic salads and roasted vegetables in earthenware bowls,
to burgers, tacos, and sundaes. Located on a corner plot, the restaurant
itself is a large, open, plant-filled space bathed in natural light. Furnishings
are simple and set within a natural color scheme. The restaurant motto
is a quote from Hippocrates: "Let food be thy medicine and medicine thy
food." Sourcing many ingredients from local organic farms — including
Farmacy's own biodynamic vegetable garden in Kent — is something owner
Camilla Fayed and her team take very seriously indeed.

The restaurant's attractive
facade on a corner site
in London's Notting Hill.

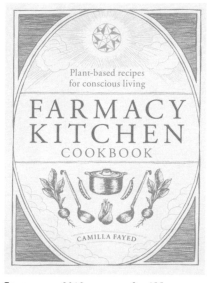

A dresser filled with herbs, homemade pickles,
and sprouted beans, many of which are grown in the
restaurant's kitchen garden.

In summer 2018, owner Camilla
Fayed launched the Farmacy Kitchen
Cookbook, packed with plant-based
recipes inspired by dishes from
around the globe.

INTO THE WOODS

HYLTEBRUK, SWEDEN

STEDSANS IN THE WOODS OFFERS GUESTS A HOLISTIC 24-HOUR CULINARY EXPERIENCE IN AN IDYLLIC SETTING IN THE SWEDISH WILDERNESS

237

When you are a restaurateur and you live by the mantra that eating food and being close to nature can change the world for the better, how do you go about creating this experience for your guests? For couple Mette Helbæk and Flemming Hansen, the answer was to create Stedsans in the Woods, an extraordinary place located in the forests of Halland, Sweden, a mere three-hour drive from their hometown, Copenhagen. "Stedsans" translates as "sense of place" in Danish and, fittingly, so, it may take some driving on dirt roads and perhaps even getting lost along the way. However, as soon as you arrive at Stedsans and discover the greenhouse restaurant, floating sauna on the lake, and the several Bedouin tents and wood cabins, your everyday life at home will quickly be forgotten. As Flemming explains, this precise location in the woods is crucial to the special ambience of Stedsans: "The place means everything. When planning the week's menu we look at what we can forage and what's in our fields. We always start with food meters instead of food miles. Then we talk to local game butchers, fishermen from the local lakes, and veggie growers. Except from salt and pepper, wine, coffee, chocolate, etc., everything comes from within one hour from Stedsans. Within this distance we hit four climate zones, three big rivers, many lakes, gigantic forests, the ocean, two permaculture farms, and three organic dairies.... It is a very special place."

Stedsans in the Woods offers a completely unique outdoor culinary experience. Somehow, Mette and

On arrival, guests are guided by simple hand-painted signage fixed to a wooden post—plain and simple.

Herbs grown in the site's permaculture farm are a major feature in the dishes served at Stedsans.

"WHEN PLANNING
THE WEEK'S MENU,
WE LOOK AT
WHAT WE CAN FORAGE
AND WHAT'S
IN OUR FIELDS."

Guests—usually more accustomed
to fine dining in the heart of the
city—enjoy the thrill of eating
semi-alfresco deep in the woods.

The large, outdoor kitchen is a
hub of activity throughout the
day and uses open fire as its only
heat source.

Flemming have managed to provide a luxurious experience in the woods. Not necessarily in the traditional sense of the word, but with their pride of place, high ambitions, Flemming's scrumptious cooking, and Mette's attention to detail in the interior design of the cabins, tents, and greenhouse. Opening a resort in the woods has been a lifelong dream, and Flemming explains how he feels cooking with local ingredients, being self-sufficient, and promoting permaculture to their guests allows him to combat the problems in the world: "Instead of spending (too much) time debating whether a sustainable life is possible, we show it to our guests and to the media around the world. We say that if a picture says more than a thousand words, a Stedsans experience says more than a thousand pictures. What tastes better is better for our surroundings and for our well-being. It is a win-win-win situation. We can change the world just by eating good food and feeling good. Our leaders won't do it for us, so we can just as well start now."

Flemming and Mette's food is fresh and simple. They prepare all their dishes on the day they are served, "à la minute," as Flemming puts it. They run an off-the-grid kitchen, using no electricity, which is only possible because of the freshness of the food. Guests arrive in the afternoon, meet the other guests, then share a beautiful, simple meal of fresh and local ingredients served family-style on communal tables. Then they leave the next day having spent a night under the stars

Weekend visitors from the city overnight in lakeside cabins. There is also a floating sauna (below), and an outdoor spa area.

ON ARRIVING AT THE GREENHOUSE RESTAURANT, YOUR EVERYDAY LIFE AT HOME IS QUICKLY FORGOTTEN.

and having shared a special experience close to nature. As Flemming explains, "It is a 24-hour experience. That means that people start talking and become friends. It is a full experience that really inspires a lot of people. Every weekend people who thought they had everything come and tell us that they want to move into the woods and start growing themselves."

By inspiring city visitors to a more holistic life in the woods, Mette and Flemming live and breath the sustainable concept of Stedsans in the Woods: to be in surroundings that are as natural as possible—surroundings that encourage contemplation, deep breathing, eating, and enjoyment. Not because it is it is the fashionable thing to do, but simply because it creates an unforgettable experience. Deep in the woods of Halland, the couple has created a haven for lovers of both simple food and the outdoors and welcomes anyone to come join them in the woods for a 24-hour culinary experience.

Before establishing Stedsans in the Woods, Mette Helbæk and Flemming Hansen ran a restaurant on the rooftop of an urban farm in Copenhagen.

"WE CAN CHANGE THE WORLD JUST BY EATING GOOD FOOD AND FEELING GOOD. IT IS A WIN-WIN-WIN SITUATION."

The chefs harvest wild mushrooms, flowers, and edible moss and grow their own fruit and vegetables.

A delicious dish of salad leaves with wild mushrooms and raspberries.

NOMA 2.0

by Studio David Thulstrup

Eleven separate buildings house the new Noma restaurant, which is designed with simplicity using custom-made furniture and carefully chosen vintage pieces.

With the reopening of the four-time "world's best restaurant," local design studio David Thulstrup has focused on the sense of place and has carefully chosen materials in close collaboration with chef René Redzepi. The yearlong process involved building the entire space from scratch, treating every wall and surface, and custom designing the furniture. The feel is Scandinavian, without being over-designed or depending on the typical Nordic clichés. Noma 2.0 now also boasts its own farm adjacent to the restaurant. There is also a platform on the adjacent lake where vegetables are grown on a floating field. The most significant change to the new menu is the way in which the restaurant now reflects the seasons of the year: seafood in winter and spring, vegetables in summer and early fall, and game and forest mushrooms in fall and winter.

Throughout the restaurant, the rooms are decorated with magnificent aquatic
species, some dried and suspended from the rafters, others pickled in glass jars.

The interior is warm and minimalist, a wholesome blend of fine oak furniture and natural stone walls.

Diners sit on mid-century-style Danish chairs with woven seats, and some are seated at chunky, rough-hewn wooden tables.

The designers at studio David Thulstrup have taken care to achieve a perfect balance of texture and scale. A chunky counter fashioned from charred logs is set against fine-grained oak paneling.

LA MÉNAGÈRE

by q-bic

La Ménagère restaurant has a variety of different functions that are tied together by the overall interior design of the rustic, nineteenth-century building.

This lofty, open-plan space in Florence combines a flower shop, music venue, cocktail bar, café, and restaurant. The spacious venue, originally a part of a home, has been revitalized by local design office q-bic, which, with great respect for the original building, has kept as many original features as possible, such as the exposed masonry columns and ceiling vaults. Guests are served at wooden tables, beneath hanging plants and a domed skylight that floods the space with natural light. There is a grand piano in the corner of the restaurant where musicians play live music. Trained at the Istituto Alberghiero Saffi, a highly reputed culinary school in Florence, chef Fabio Barbaglini guarantees an imaginative and innovative experience with his fine Italian cuisine.

The main restaurant is awash with rustic charm, with its eclectic collection of pendant lights and shelves lined with pots and plants adding to the menagerie feel of the place.

In homage to the building's nineteenth-century history, the menu is ornamented with Victorian engravings of culinary otifs.

(right) Among the delights at La Ménagère is this elongated dining room, ideal for celebrations and private gatherings.

INDEX

21 gramm
21gramm.berlin
Berlin, Germany
pp. 164–167
Photography:
Jules Villbrandt

Aimo e Nadia BistRo
bistroaimoenadia.com
Milan, Italy
pp. 158–161
Photography:
Brambilla Serrani
Interior Design:
Rossana Orlandi

Amass Restaurant
amassrestaurant.com
Copenhagen, Denmark
pp. 199–200 (top)
Photography:
Mikkel Heriba

Astair
astair.paris
Paris, France
pp. 134–137
Photography:
Vincent Leroux

Atoboy
atoboynyc.com
New York, USA
pp. 112–113
Photography:
Courtesy of Atoboy

Babel
babylonstoren.com
Paarl, South Africa
pp. 4, 196, 210–215
Photography:
Courtesy of Babylonstoren

Bad Taste
badtaste.biz
New York, USA
p. 70
Photography: Steven Acres

Bazaar Mar
thebazaar.com
Miami, USA
pp. 230–231
Photography: Eric Laignel

Benedict
benedict-breakfast.de
Berlin, Germany
pp. 32–33
Photography:
Markus Braumann

Big Mamma
bigmammagroup.com
Paris, France
pp. 118–125
Photography:
pp. 118, 121, 124 (bottom),
p. 125 Jérôme Galland,
p. 120 (bottom) Fabien
Breuil, p. 120 (top), p. 122
(bottom), p. 124 (top)
Joann Pai, p. 122 (top),
p. 123 Sabri Beny

Bo.lan
bolan.co.th
Bangkok, Thailand
pp. 126, 132, 133
Photography:
Courtesy of Bo.lan

Crème de la Crème
cremedelacreme.at
Vienna, Austria
pp. 162–163
Photography:
Mike Rabensteiner
Interior Design:
Alex Riegler
Graphic Design:
Bureau Rabensteiner

Casaplata
Seville, Spain
pp. 74–77
Photography: Juan Delgado
Architecture:
Lucas y Hernández-Gil
Furniture and lighting:
Kresta Design

China Chilcano
chinachilcano.com
Washington D.C., USA
pp. 180–181
Photography:
p. 180 Ken Wyner,
p. 181 Greg Powers

Deus Ex Machina
deuscustoms.com
Los Angeles, USA, Sydney,
Australia, Milan, Italy,
Tokyo, Japan, Bali,
Indonesia

pp. 58–65
Photography:
Jason No & Nevin Pontious

Doot Doot Doot &
Flaggerdoot
jackalopehotels.com
Melbourne, Australia
pp. 114–117
Photography:
pp. 114, 116, 117 (top &
bottom left) Sharyn Cairns,
pp. 115, 117 (bottom right)
Jason Loucas, p. 117 (top
right) Rick Liston

Dragsholm Slot
dragsholm-slot.dk
Zealand, Denmark
pp. 168–175
Photography:
p. 168, 169, 171,
172 (bottom) Claus Starup,
169 (left), 174 (bottom)
Ida Ejdrup Nielsen,
170 (top), 171 (top and
bottom right) Kirstine
Fryd, 170 (bottom),
172 (top) Jacob Termansen,
172 (bottom) Claes
Bech-Poulsen, 173 Henrik
Saxgren, 174 (top)
Per-Anders Jörgensen,
175 Michael Jepsen

Duddell's
duddells.co/london
London, U.K.
pp. 138–139
Photography: Ed Reeve

Eatrip
restaurant-eatrip.com
Tokyo, Japan
pp. 34–41
Photography: Aya Brackett

Egg Kneipe
eggkneipe.de
Berlin, Germany
pp. 102–105
Photography: Courtesy of
Egg Kneipe/Kristof Kozma

Farmacy
farmacylondon.com
London, U.K.
pp. 200, 232–235
Photography:
Courtesy of Farmacy

Fotografiska Restaurant
fotografiska.com
Stockholm, Sweden
pp. 129, 201
Photography:
Jenny Hammar

Graanmarkt 13
graanmarkt13.com
Antwerp, Belgium
pp. 226–229
Photography:
Jessica Jungbauer

Incredible Edible
incredibleedible.org.uk
Bristol, London and
Salford, U.K.
p. 10
Photography:
Courtesy of
Incredible Edible

JUST
justforall.com
San Francisco, USA
p. 71
Photography:
Courtesy of JUST

Kajitsu
kajitsunyc.com
New York, USA
pp. 186–195
Photography: Nathan Bajar
Additional Credit:
From The New York Times,
(25/07), © (2018)
The New York Times.
All rights reserved.
Used by permission and
protected by the Copyright
Laws of the United States.
The printing, copying,
redistribution, or retrans-
mission of this Content
without express written
permission is prohibited.

Kiin Kiin Bao Bao
kiinbao.dk
Copenhagen, Denmark
pp. 216–217
Photography:
Henrik Freek Christensen

KitchenTown
kitchentowncentral.com
San Francisco Bay Area,
USA
Photography:
pp. 14, 90–95
pp. 14, 90, 91, 93 Molly De
Coudreaux, 95 (top left
& right) Blue Evolution,
(middle right & bottom
right) ReGrained,
(bottom left) Lisa Vortman

La Colmada
lacolmada.com
Madrid, Spain
pp. 146–149
Photography:

Courtesy of La Colmada
Graphic Design:
Ultramarina Studio

La Ménagère
lamenagere.it
Florence, Italy
pp. 250–253
Photography:
Mino Pasqualone

La REcyclerie
larecyclerie.com
Paris, France
pp. 28–31
Photography: pp. 28–31
Sion Le Marchand, p. 30
(top left) La REcyclerie

Legacy Records
legacyrecordsrestaurant.com
New York, USA
pp. 54–57
Photography:
Douglas Friedman
Interior Design: Ken Fulk

Lina Stores
linastores.co.uk
London, U.K.
pp. 130, 150–157
Photography:
pp. 130 (bottom), 150, 151
(left), 153 (left & bottom
right), 155, 156 (bottom
right), 157 Mariell Lind
Hansen, pp. 151 (right),
152, 153 (top right),
154, 156 (top right &
bottom left) Hugh Johnson

MIL Centro
milcentro.pe
Cusco, Peru
pp. 15, 218–225
Photography:
Gustavo Vivanco

Mosquito Supper Club
mosquitosupperclub.com
New Orleans, USA
pp. 131, 176–179
Photography:
Jillian Greenberg

Naim
naimrestaurant.com.au
Brisbane, Australia /
Brighton, U.K.
pp. 7, 78–79
Photography:
Sean Fennessey
Interior Design:
The Stella Collective

Noma 2.0
noma.dk

Denmark, Copenhagen
pp. 244–249
Photography:
Irina Boersma

Pastéis de Belém
pasteisdebelem.pt
Lisbon, Portugal
p. 128
Photography: Courtesy of
Pastéis de Belém

Patent Pending
patentpendingnyc.com
New York, NY
pp. 182–185
Photography:
Jacob Williamson
Creative: Ryan McKenzie

Piada
piadafood.com
Lyon, France
pp. 44–47
Photography: Luis Beltrán
Design: Masquespacio
Architect:
Sandrine Brenans

Pink Zebra
studiorenesa.com
Kanpur, India
pp. 106–111
Photography:
Suryan / Dang

Poke Poke
Shanghai, China
pp. 98–101
Photography: M2STUDIO
Architecture: Studio Doho
Graphic Design:
Katherine Szeto

Prado Restaurante
pradorestaurante.com
Lisbon, Portugal
pp. 140–145
Photography:
Rodrigo Cardoso
Interior Design:
Arkstudio

Prossima Fermata
Milan, Italy
pp. 96–97
Photography:
Federico Villa studio
Architecture: Studio Wok
Wood carpenter:
Arredo 90 srl
Terrazzo: Marmi scala
Linoleum: Forbo

QO Amsterdam
qo-amsterdam.com
Amsterdam,

The Netherlands
p. 71 (top), 80–85, 198
Photography:
Rinze Vegelien
Interior Design: TANK

Relæ
restaurant-relae.dk
Copenhagen, Denmark
pp. 202 (top)–203
Photography:
P.A. Jorgensen

Ryú
ryusushi.ca
Montreal, Canada
pp. 48–53
Photography:
pp. 48, 50 (bottom right),
51, 52 (top right),
53 David Dworkind,
pp. 49, 50 (top left,
top right & bottom right)
Saria Chatila
Interior Design:
Ménard Dworkind
Architecture & Design

Salad Jungle
saladjungle.at
Vienna, Austria
pp. 208–209
Photography:
Courtesy of Salad Jungle

Sala Equis
salaequis.es
Madrid, Spain
pp. 16–19
Photography:
Lucía Marcano
Architecture: Plantea

SPACE10
space10.io
Copenhagen, Denmark
pp. 66, 68, 69, 70, 73
Photography:
pp. 66, 68 (top), 69,
70 (top), 73 Kasper
Kristoffersen,
68 (bottom) Rory Gardiner

Spiritland
spiritland.com
London, U.K.
pp. 20–21
Photography:
Adam Scott
Architecture:
Fraher Architects

Stedsans
in the Woods
stedsans.org
Hyltebruk, Denmark
pp. 236–243

Photography:
pp. 236, 237,
238, 239, 240, 241,
242 (bottom right),
243 Stine Christiansen,
p. 242 (bottom right)
Inge Skovdal

St. JOHN Restaurant
stjohnrestaurant.com
London, U.K.
pp. 129–130
Photography:
p. 129 (top)
Stefan Johnson,
p. 130 (top)
Patricia Niven

Tacofino Oasis
tacofino.com
Vancouver, Canada
pp. 86–89
Photography:
Vishal Marapon
Designer: Shiloh Sukkau
Contractor: Pacific
Solutions Contracting
Graphic Design:
Courtney Presber
Styling: Mila Franovic

The Blind Donkey
theblinddonkey.jp
Tokyo, Japan
pp. 13, 22–27
Photography:
Kohei Take

Über den Tellerrand
ueberdentellerrand.org
Berlin, Germany
pp. 8, 11, 12, 14
Photography:
Courtesy of
Über den Tellerrand

Väkst
cofoco.dk/en/restaurants/
vaekst
Copenhagen, Denmark
pp. 204–207
Photography:
Chris Tonnesen

Vollpension
vollpension.wien
Vienna, Austria
pp. 10, 42–43
Photography:
Mark Glassner

Zur Letzten Instanz
zurletzteninstanz.com
Berlin, Germany
p. 128
Photography: Courtesy of
Zur Letzen Instanz

Delicious
Places

New Food Culture,
Restaurants, and Interiors

This book was conceived, edited,
and designed by gestalten.

Edited by Robert Klanten
and Anja Kouznetsova

Preface by James Clasper
Texts written by Anna Southgate,
Nana Hagel (pp. 58–65, 80–85, 90–95, 118–125,
196–203, 216–217, 218–225, 244–253),
Jessica Jungbauer (pp. 8–15, 66–73, 126–133),
Ben Ratcliff (pp. 186–195)

Editorial Management by Sam Stevenson

Design by Hy-Ran Kilian

Typefaces: Times New Roman by
Stanley Morison (Linotype)
and Lars Mono by Mads Wildgaard
(Bold Decisions)

Cover photography by Vishal Marapon
Backcover photography by
Aya Brackett (top left),
Babylonstoren (top right),
La Colmada (bottom left),
and Sean Fennessey (bottom right)

Printed by Nino Druck GmbH,
Neustadt/Weinstraße
Made in Germany

Published by gestalten, Berlin 2019
ISBN 978-3-89955-969-9

For more information, and to order books, please visit
www.gestalten.com.

Bibliographic information published by the
Deutsche Nationalbibliothek.
The Deutsche Nationalbibliothek lists this publication
in the Deutsche Nationalbibliografie;
detailed bibliographic data are available online at
www.dnb.de

None of the content in this book was published in
exchange for payment by commercial parties or designers;
gestalten selected all included work based solely
on its artistic merit.

This book was printed on paper certified according to the
standards of the FSC®.

DATE DUE
